Favor
AIN'T FAIR

DESTINY IMAGE BOOKS BY T.D. JAKES

T.D. JAKES

Favor AIN'T FAIR

90 PROMISES FOR EXPERIENCING GOD'S BLESSING, ABUNDANCE, AND PROVISION

DESTINY IMAGE® PUBLISHERS, INC.
P.O. Box 310, Shippensburg, PA 17257-0310

"Publishing cutting-edge prophetic resources to supernaturally empower the body of Christ"

This book and all other Destiny Image and Destiny Image Fiction books are available at Christian bookstores and distributors worldwide.

For more information on foreign distributors, call 717-532-3040.

Reach us on the Internet: www.destinyimage.com.

ISBN 13 TP: 978-0-7684-7658-3

ISBN 13 eBook: 978-0-7684-7659-0

For Worldwide Distribution, Printed in the U.S.A.

1 2 3 4 5 6 7 8 / 28 27 26 25 24

Contents

Introduction

THROUGHOUT THE BIBLE, many sought and received God's favor—from Jacob (Genesis 33:10) to Joseph for his brother Benjamin (Genesis 43:29), Moses (Exodus 32:11), King Manasseh (2 Chronicles 33:12), and Daniel (Daniel 1:9) to the Lord of Hosts (Malachi 1:9) to Mary the mother of Jesus (Luke 1:30) and to Jesus Himself (Luke 2:52), among others.

God wants to bestow His favor upon all His children. Divine favor is the supernatural agent that positions us for "unfair" blessings, abundance, and provision. We are to assume our right and privilege to sit at the King's table and receive our divine inheritance—as a result, a blessing, a benefit of becoming children of God through the sacrifice and shed blood of His Son, Jesus.

The key to knowing your purpose is celebrating your *personal* identity by discovering that you have been uniquely gifted to fulfill a divine calling. In a worldly context, favor is usually given to those who gain a special liking because of their education, family roots, intellect, appearance, any number of attributes that the world admires.

But in God's Kingdom, favor is showered over believers who may have committed murders, cheated on their spouses, abandoned their families, were thieves, conspired to betray—any number of criminal and/or immoral acts. How can this be?

God sent His Son, Jesus, to wipe away sin and usher in forgiveness for those who acknowledge His sovereignty and sacrifice on the Cross—for those who realize His blood covers all sin once and for all for the repentant sinner.

Says Saul (a Christian persecutor), now Paul the apostle: *"But whatever I am now, it is all because **God poured out his special favor** on me—and not without results. For I have worked harder than any of the other apostles; yet it was not I but God who was working through me by his grace"* (1 Corinthians 15:10 NLT).

In this journey through the next 90 days of God's promises, you will see how His generosity for you has no boundaries. No matter your background, race, age, social standing, education, or bank account balance, God sees you only as His child, whom He loves unconditionally.

> *So it is right that I should feel as I do about all of you, for you have a special place in my heart. **You share with me the special favor of God**, both in my imprisonment and in defending and confirming the truth of the Good News* (Philippians 1:7 NLT).

You are encouraged to receive each of God's promises as your very own. Meditate on each one as if He wrote it into the Bible just for you—because He did!

> *Never let loyalty and kindness leave you! Tie them around your neck as a reminder. Write them deep within your heart. Then **you will find favor with both God and people**, and you will earn a good reputation* (Proverbs 3:3-4 NLT).

It is so important for you to invest your heart, time, resources, and energies into harvesting the good fruit that comes from His favor—that you will discover through His promises!

> If you pray to God and **seek the favor of the Almighty**, and if you are pure and live with integrity, he will surely rise up and restore your happy home (Job 8:5-6 NLT).

God Will Fulfill His Promises

*Being confident of this very thing, that **He who has begun a good work in you will complete it until the day of Jesus Christ*** (Philippians 1:6 NKJV).

IN GENESIS, THE LORD PROMISED Eve a seed, saying, *"And I will cause hostility between you and the woman, and between your offspring and her offspring. He will strike your head, and you will strike his heel"* (Genesis 3:15 NLT). When Eve produced what she may have thought to be the promised seed, there were real problems. In the heat of rage, Cain killed his brother. Now her elder son was a criminal on the run, and her younger son was snuffed out in the prime of life. She was supposed to be the mother of all living, and all she had raised was a corpse and its murderer.

But God unwrapped the blanket of failure from around her and blessed her with another son. She called him Seth, which means "substituted." Suddenly, as she held her new baby in her arms, she began to realize that God is sovereign. If He decrees a thing, it will surely come to pass. Eve called her third son Seth because she understood that when *God makes a promise to bless someone, He will find a way!* Even if it means appointing a substitute, *He will fulfill His promise.*

God's purpose was not aborted when Cain killed Abel. In spite of the fact that life has its broken places, ultimately everything God has ever said will come to pass. Satan tries to assassinate the will of God in your life. Nevertheless, God has begun a good work in you—and He will complete it!

When we suffer loss like Eve did, there is a feeling of forlornness. However, you can't allow past circumstances to abort future opportunity. If you have experienced loss in your life, I tell you that God has a way of restoring what you thought you would never see again.

Prayer

Heavenly Father, thank You for the promise of restoration. I claim this promise for my very own and give You all the praise and glory—for all is Yours and more. In the precious name of Jesus, amen.

Declaration

God will restore what the evil one has stolen!

Faith to Wait

Wait patiently for the Lord. Be brave and courageous.
Yes, wait patiently for the Lord (Psalm 27:14 NLT).

IT IS GOD'S TIMING that we must learn. He synchronizes His answers to accomplish His purpose. Recently, while traveling on a major American airline, we were told that the plane could not land at its scheduled time. Evidently the air traffic controller instructed that we should wait in the air. What a strange place to have to wait—in the air!

I have often felt like that aircraft suspended in the air when God says, "Wait!" Then the captain spoke into the PA system. He said, "We are going to assume a holding pattern until further instructions come from the tower." After some time, a few rather intoxicated passengers began to question the traffic controller's decision. Perhaps we were all concerned. It's just that some had their concern lubricated with several stiff shots of rum!

The anxious looks and acidic remarks that came from the crowd subsided as the stewardess quickly eased people's fears. She informed several worried passengers that the planes always carry enough fuel to withstand the demands of these kinds of delays. There was a calm assurance on the faces of the attendants. I would have to attribute it to the fact that they had prepared for a delay.

I began to wonder if we as the children of God shouldn't be better prepared for those times in our lives when God speaks from His throne, "Assume a holding pattern until further notice." The question is not always, "Do you have enough faith to receive?" Sometimes it is, "Do you have enough faith to assume a holding pattern and wait for the fulfillment of the promise?" You feel a deep sense of contentment when you know God has not forgotten you.

I will never forget the time I went through a tremendous struggle. I thought it was an emergency. I thought I had to have an answer right then. I learned that God isn't easily spooked by what I call an emergency.

Prayer

Lord God, You are always in control—may my faith and life reflect that truth in my everyday living, as well as during "holding patterns." Strengthen me, Lord, while I wait for the fulfillment of every promise You have designed for my future. In Jesus's name, amen.

Declaration

I will wait patiently for the Lord! I will be brave and courageous!

God Remembers

God is not unjust; he will not forget your work and the love you have shown him as you have helped his people and continue to help them (Hebrews 6:10 NIV).

ONCE WHILE STRUGGLING in my heart to understand why God had not more readily answered one of my requests, I stumbled upon a word that brought streams into my desert.

> **But God remembered** *Noah and all the wild animals and the livestock that were with him in the ark, and he sent a wind over the earth, and the waters receded* (Genesis 8:1 NIV).

The first three words were all I needed. I still quote them from time to time.

When you realize that God knows where you are and that He will get back to you in time—what peace, what joy! Before Noah ran out of resources and provisions, God remembered him! The Lord knows where you are, and He knows how much you have left in reserve. Just before you run out, God will send the wind to blow back the waters of impossibility and provide for you.

I can't begin to describe the real ammunition I received out of those powerful words: *But God remembered Noah!* I, too, need ministry to keep my attitude from falling while I wait on the manifestation of the promise of God. Sometimes very simplistic reminders that God is still sovereign bring great joy to the heart of someone who is in a holding pattern.

The comforting Spirit of God calms my fears every time He reminds me that God doesn't forget. When working with people, we often must remind them that we are still there. They seem to readily forget who we are or what we did. God doesn't!

Don't confuse your relationship with Him with your relationship with people. God says, through Paul, that it is unrighteous to forget. God simply doesn't forget. He has excellent records.

Prayer

Dear God of Promises, thank You for never forgetting me, for always remembering where I am and how much provision I have left. Out of Your abundance, You share Your love and blessings, for which I am grateful. In the glorious name of Your Son, Jesus, amen.

Declaration

I will stand firm on the promise that God will remember me—no matter what!

God's Mighty Rushing Wind

*And suddenly there came a sound from heaven,
as of a rushing mighty wind, and it filled the whole
house where they were sitting* (Acts 2:2 NKJV).

GOD'S RECORDS ARE SO COMPLETE that the hairs on your head are numbered (see Matthew 10:30). They are not just counted. *Counted* would mean He simply knows how many. No, they are *numbered,* meaning He knows which hair is in your comb! You should know He has chronological records of your hair strands. You should also know He has your family, your tithes, and your faithfulness in His view. How much more could God watch over you, if He already watches the numerical order of your hair? No wonder David declares, *"What are mere mortals that you should think about them, human beings that you should care for them?"* (Psalm 8:4 NLT).

My friend, God's mind is full of you. Even in those moments of absolute stagnation in your life, He is working an expected end for your good (see Jeremiah 29:11). When Noah had been held up long enough to accomplish what was necessary for his good, God sent the wind. There is a wind that comes from the presence of God. It blows back the hindrances and dries the ground beneath your feet. The wind of the Holy Spirit often comes as a sign to you from the control tower. You have been cleared for a landing!

Whenever the breath of the Almighty breathes a fresh anointing on you, it is a divine indication of a supernatural deliverance. Regardless of the obstacles in your life, there is a wind from God that can bring you out. Let the wind of the Lord blow down every spirit of fear and heaviness that would cause you to give up on what God has promised you.

The description of the Holy Spirit says He is as "a rushing mighty wind" (Acts 2:2). For every mighty problem in your life, there is a mighty rushing wind! Now, a normal wind can be blocked out. If you close the door and lock the windows, the wind just passes over without changing the building.

But if the wind is a mighty rushing wind, it will blow down the door and break in the windows. There is a gusty wind from the Lord that is too strong to be controlled. It will blow back the Red Sea. It will roll back the Jordan River. It will blow dry the wet, marshy, flooded lands as in the days of Noah. God's wind is still ultra-effective against every current event in your life.

Prayer

Holy Spirit, blow Yourself into my life—break off the sin that has been too long an intruder. Break the windows of unforgiveness, jealousy, and anger—replacing each with forgiveness, love, and mercy. I welcome Your gusty winds, knowing that with them is Your promise of Your Spirit within me, guiding me into Your arms.

Declaration

I will listen carefully for the
Controller in the tower clearing me
for a safe and sound landing!

Escape

Anger gives a foothold to the devil (Ephesians 4:27 NLT).

IT IS NOT ENOUGH to *reject* the enemy's plan. You must *nurture* the Word of the Lord. You need to draw the promise of God and the vision for the future to you. It is a natural law that anything not fed will die. Whatever you have drawn to you is what is growing in your life. Breastfeeding holds several advantages for what you feed: (1) it hears your heart beat, (2) it is warmed by your closeness, and (3) it draws nourishment from you. Caution: Be sure you are nurturing what you want to grow and starving what you want to die.

As you read this, you may feel that life is passing you by. You may often experience success in one area and gross defeat in others. You need a burning desire for the future, the kind of desire that overcomes past fear and inhibitions. You will remain chained to your past and all the secrets therein until you decide: Enough is enough! I am telling you that when your desire for the future peaks, you can break out of any prison.

I challenge you to sit down and write 30 things you would like to do with your life, and scratch them off, one by one, as you accomplish them. There is no way you can plan for the future and dwell in the past at the same time.

I feel an earthquake coming into your prison! It is midnight—the turning point of days! It is your time for a change. Praise God and escape out of the dungeons of your past.

Around midnight Paul and Silas were praying and singing hymns to God, and the other prisoners were listening. Suddenly, there was a massive earthquake, and the prison was shaken to its foundations. All the doors immediately flew open, and the chains of every prisoner fell off! (Acts 16:25-26 NLT).

Prayer

Heavenly Father, for too long I have been held captive by my past—but no longer. With Your help, I will break free by feeding only what is good and nutritious in my life. I will starve off negativity and sin—placing You and Your promises firmly in the middle of everything I say and do and believe. Thank You for my freedom, Jesus!

Declaration

**Today I will give no room to the devil—
God reigns wholeheartedly in my life!**

Freedom

But the Scriptures declare that we are all prisoners of sin, so we receive God's promise of freedom only by believing in Jesus Christ (Galatians 3:22 NLT).

MANY CHRISTIANS experienced the new birth early in their childhood. It is beneficial to have the advantage of Christian ethics. I'm not sure what it would have been like to be raised in the Church and insulated from worldliness and sin. Sometimes I envy those who have been able to live victoriously all of their lives. Most of us have not had that kind of life.

My concern is the many persons who have lost their sensitivity for others and who suffer from spiritual arrogance. Jesus condemned the Pharisees for their spiritual arrogance, yet many times that self-righteous spirit creeps into churches. There are those who define holiness as what someone wears or what a person eats. For years churches displayed the name "holiness" because they monitored a person's outward appearance. They weren't truly looking at character. Often they were carried away with whether someone should wear makeup or jewelry when thousands of people were destroying themselves on drugs and prostitution. Priorities were confused. Unchurched people who came to church had no idea why the minister would emphasize outward apparel when people were bleeding inside.

The fact is, we were all born in sin and shaped in iniquity. We have no true badge of righteousness that we can wear on the outside. God concluded all are in sin so He may save us from ourselves (see Galatians 3:22). It wasn't the act of sin but the state of sin that brought us into condemnation. We were born in sin, equally and individually shaped in iniquity, and not one race or sociological group has escaped the fact that we are Adam's sinful heritage.

Prayer

Dear God, as the great hymn confirms, "Amazing grace, how sweet the sound that saved a wretch like me." Thank You for saving this wretch, this sinner—yet this child of Yours. I look forward, Lord, to those ten thousand years of singing Your praise—and then ten thousand more. Thank You for salvation through Your Son, Jesus. Amen.

Declaration

Because I believe in Jesus, I have and claim and welcome God's promise of freedom!

Peace

*I will comfort you there in Jerusalem as a
mother comforts her child* (Isaiah 66:13 NLT).

I REMEMBER WHEN our car broke down. It didn't have too
far to break down because it already was at death's door. The
only way to fix that car was to commit the body to the ground
and give the engine to the Lord.

At the time, though, I needed to get uptown to ask the
electric company not to cut off the only utility I had left. I
caught the bus to town. I walked into the office prepared to
beg—but not prepared to pay. I pleaded with the young lady;
I promised her money. Nothing seemed to move her, and she
cut it off anyway. I was crushed. I had been laid off my job,
and my church was so poor it couldn't even pay attention. I
was in trouble.

I walked out of the utility office and burst into tears. I don't
mean the quiet leaking of the tear ducts either. I mean a deluge of sobbing, heaving, quaking, and wailing. I looked like
an insane person walking down the street. I was at the end
of my rope.

To this melodramatic outburst God said absolutely nothing.
He waited until I had gained some slight level of composure
and then spoke. I will never forget the sweet sound of His
voice beneath the broken breathing of my fearful frustration.
He said, in the rich tones of a clarinet-type voice, "I will not

suffer thy foot to be moved!" That was all He said, but it was how He said it that caused worship to flush the pain out of my heart. It was as if He were saying, "Who do you think that I am? I will not suffer thy foot to be moved. Don't you understand that I love you?"

I shall never forget as long as I live the holy hush and the peace of His promise that came into my spirit. Suddenly the lights, the gas, and the money didn't matter. What mattered was I knew I was not alone. He sat down beside me, and we rode home smiling in each other's face. It was the Lord and I.

Prayer

Oh Lord, my sweet Companion and Savior, how can I ever doubt Your faithfulness and presence? Your comfort and peace flood my being—when I listen for Your voice rather than dwell on my frustrations and fears. Father, thank You for always saying the right thing at the right time to calm my emotions. In Jesus's name, amen.

Declaration

I will make it a habit to listen more closely for God's soothing voice rather than my raging emotions.

No Broken Promises

He rescued me from my powerful enemies, from those who hated me and were too strong for me. They attacked me at a moment when I was in distress, but the Lord supported me. He led me to a place of safety; he rescued me because he delights in me (Psalm 18:17-19 NLT).

THERE IS A DEEP-SEATED NEED in all of us to sense purpose—even out of calamity. Out of this thirst for meaning is born the simplistic yet crucial prayer, "Why?" Many times we want to know and understand. It is part of our superior creative ability. It separates us from lower forms of life that tend to accept events as they come. There is within us this insatiable need to understand.

On the other hand, we seem to draw some degree of solace from our very quest to know why. No matter how painful the quest, we will still search through the rubbish of broken dreams, broken promises, and twisted childhood issues looking for clues. We ambitiously pursue these clues because we believe there is a reward for the discovery. This emotional autopsy often takes us through the bowels of human attitudes and dysfunctional behavior. We don't have to necessarily erase the cause of our pain; we mainly just want to find some reason or justification for the pain and discomfort.

"Then Jacob was left alone; and a Man wrestled with him until the breaking of day" (Genesis 32:24 NKJV). Like Jacob,

everyone knows what it means to be left alone. Whether through death, desertion, or even disagreement, we have all been left alone at times. We are sometimes disillusioned when we find out how easily people will leave us. Generally, they leave us when we think that we need them.

This may be difficult, but it is all part of God's "scholastic achievement program" for strong believers. He is determined to strip us of our strong tendency to be dependent on others, thereby teaching us self-reliance and God-reliance. Thus the struggle truly begins not when people surround us—but rather when they forsake us. It is then when we begin to discover our own identity and self-worth!

It is unrealistic to expect no pain when there is disappointment or rejection. No matter how spiritual we may be, when covenants are broken and trust is betrayed, even the most stoic person will wince at the pain!

Prayer

My Lord and Savior, how reassuring it is to know You will never leave me or forsake me. You are the Promise Keeper—not a promise breaker. I know this in my spirit, and I trust You implicitly to follow through with Your promise—and I promise to give You all the glory for every good thing that happens in my life. In Jesus's name, amen.

Declaration

I am rescued from powerful enemies because the Lord supports me. He leads me to safety because He delights in me.

Freedom from Every Curse

Rescue the weak and the needy; deliver them from the hand of the wicked (Psalm 82:4 NIV).

THE ENEMY WANTS TO violate God's children. He is planning and plotting your destruction. He has watched you with wanton eyes. He has great passion and perseverance. Jesus told Peter, *"Satan has asked for you, that he may sift you as wheat. But I have prayed for you"* (Luke 22:31-32 NKJV). Satan lusts after God's children. He wants you. He craves for you with an animalistic passion. He awaits an opportunity for attack.

In addition, he loves to use people to fulfill the same kinds of lust upon one another. Desire is a motivating force. It can make you do things you never thought yourself capable of doing. Lust can make us break our commitment to ourselves. It will cause people to reach after things they never thought they would reach for.

Like Peter, you may have gone through some horrible times, but Jesus intercedes on your behalf. No matter the struggles you have faced, confidence is found in the ministry of our High Priest. He prays for you. Faith comes when you recognize that you can't help yourself. Only trust in Christ can bring you through.

Many have suffered mightily, but Christ gives the strength to overcome the attacks of satan and human, selfish lust.

Often the residual effects of being abused linger for many years. Some never find deliverance because they never allow Christ to come into the dark places of their lives.

Jesus has promised to set you free from every curse of the past. If you have suffered abuse, please know that He will bring you complete healing. He wants the whole person well—in body, emotions, and spirit. He will deliver you from all the residue of your past.

Prayer

Great Physician, I come to You as a humble, hurting child. I accept Your promise of freeing me from every curse of the past. I welcome Your healing hands of mercy. I thank You for erasing all the residue of any and all abuse—be it physical, mental, spiritual, or emotional. In You are all the glory, honor, and power. Amen.

Declaration

I am healed of past pain, hurt, anger, abuse, and all that is ungodly!

Anointing

You love righteousness and hate wickedness; therefore God, your God, has set you above your companions by anointing you with the oil of joy (Psalm 45:7 NIV).

I KNOW THIS SOUNDS OLD-FASHIONED, but I believe *anything worth doing is worth doing well.* God Himself takes His time developing us. No instant success will do. He wants to put the quality in before the name goes out. A small beginning is just the prelude to a tremendous crescendo at the finale! Many of God's masterpieces were developed in small, obscure circumstances.

Moses, the "messiah" of the Old Testament sent to the lost sheep of Israel, was trained in leadership while shoveling sheep dung on the backside of the desert. There was no fancy finishing school for this boy. Granted, his discipline was developed in the royal courts of Pharaoh's house, but his disposition was shaped through a failure in his life and a desert kingdom with no one for him to lead but flies, gnats, and sheep. Who would have thought, looking at Moses's church of goat deacons and gnats for choir members, that he later would lead the greatest movement in the history of Old Testament theology?

Who would have guessed that old impotent Abraham, whose sun had gone down and force gone out, would finally father a nation—in fact, a nationality? One moment he is sitting on the edge of the bed with an embarrassed look on his face, and the next moment he is fathering children even after Sarah's death. You can't tell what's in you by looking at you. God is establishing patience, character, and concentration in the school of "nothing seems to be happening." Take the class and get the course credit; it's working for your good.

Many misunderstand the prophecies of the Lord and so feel discontentment and despair. Just because God promises to move in your life and anoints you to do a particular function doesn't mean that your foundation will be immediately built.

Prayer

My prayer today is to realize that You, God, are working and moving in my life daily—even though it may not seem as if You are. I believe that you have anointed my life to reflect Your faithfulness and goodness. My foundation is built on You and You alone. In Your Son's name, amen.

Declaration

I am God's child. His anointing carries me through each day with joy!

Pregnancy

But the angel said to him: "Do not be afraid, Zechariah; your prayer has been heard. Your wife Elizabeth will bear you a son, and you are to call him John" (Luke 1:13 NIV).

ELIZABETH, THE WIFE OF THE PRIEST ZACHARIAH, is the biblical synonym for the modern pastor's wife. She was a winter woman with a summer experience. She was *pregnant with a promise.* In spite of her declining years, she was fulfilling more destiny *then* than she had in her youth. She is biblical proof that God blesses us in His own time and on His own terms. She was also in seclusion. Perhaps it was the attitude of the community.

Many times when an older woman is still vibrant and productive, it can cause jealousy and intimidation. Perhaps it was the silent stillness in her womb, which some believe she experienced. Whatever the reason, she was a recluse for six months until she heard a knock at the door. If you have isolated yourself from others, regardless of the reason, I pray you will hear the knocking of the Lord. He will give you the garment of praise to clothe the spirit of heaviness (see Isaiah 61:3).

When Elizabeth lifted her still-creaking body, which seemed almost anchored down to the chair, and walked her enlarged torso to the door, she saw a young girl, a picture of herself in days gone by, standing there. Opening that door changed her life forever.

As you open the door to new relationships and remove the chain from your own fears, God will overwhelm you with new splendor. Mary, the future mother of our Savior and Lord, Elizabeth's young cousin, was at the door. The salutation of this young woman, the exposure to her experience, made the baby in Elizabeth's womb leap, and Elizabeth was filled with the Holy Spirit.

God will jump-start your heart! He doesn't mean for you to go sit in a chair and die! *In Jesus's name, get up and answer the door!* People probably wondered why these women who were so different were so close, but it was a God-bond!

Prayer

Father God, I'm excited to know that I am pregnant with a promise that You have placed within me. I pray that You will prepare me to birth this promise according to Your will and that I will welcome what You have in my future, nurturing it as to Your desires. In thankfulness and praise and Jesus's name, amen.

Declaration

I will open every door of opportunity that God places in front of me!

Promised Seed

The Lord appeared to Abraham near the great trees of Mamre while he was sitting at the entrance to his tent in the heat of the day. ...Then one of them said, "I will surely return to you about this time next year, and Sarah your wife will have a son" (Genesis 18:1, 10 NIV).

Sarah became pregnant and bore a son to Abraham in his old age, at the very time God had promised him (Genesis 21:2 NIV).

BETWEEN THESE POWERFUL MOMENTS in the life of one of God's finest examples of wives, everything in Sarah was tested. I believe that her love for Abraham gave her the courage to leave home, but her love for God brought forth the promised seed.

Careful now. I'm not saying that her love for God replaced her love for her husband; I am merely saying that it complemented the other to the highest level. After all, what good is it to appreciate what God gave us if we do not appreciate the God who gave it to us? If age should do nothing else, it should help us put things in proper perspective. There is nothing like time to show us that we have misplaced priorities.

In summer, she followed Abraham out of their country and away from their kindred. As the seasons of life changed, she took another pilgrimage into what could have been a great tragedy. Abraham, her beloved husband, led his wife into Gerar. As I am a man and a leader myself, I dare not be too hard on him. Anyone can make a poor decision. The decision to go to Gerar I could defend, even though Gerar means "halting place." I have made decisions that brought me to a halting place in my life.

What's reprehensible is that Abraham, Sarah's protector and covering, when afraid for his own safety, lied about her identity (Genesis 20). You never know who people are until you witness them under pressure. Now, I am not being sanctimonious about Abraham's flagrant disregard for truth. But it was a life-threatening lie.

Prayer

All-knowing God, as You look into my future, I pray that You will have mercy on me if I make the wrong decisions. I will depend on Your wisdom to guide me when I have decisions to make, but I realize that I stumble ahead of You sometimes, leaning toward my human wants and needs rather than Your desires. I place my trust in You and Your Word. In Jesus's name, amen.

Declaration

I will lean on the Lord when making decisions—big or small!

Faith

*And what more shall I say? I do not have time to tell about Gideon, Barak, Samson and Jephthah, about David and Samuel and the prophets, **who through faith** conquered kingdoms, administered justice, and **gained what was promised**; who shut the mouths of lions* (Hebrews 11:32-33 NIV).

THE FANATICISM OF SOME theologies has intimidated many Christians from faith concepts as they relate to the promises of God. Yet faith is such a key issue for the Christian that the people of the early Church were simply called "believers" in recognition of their great faith.

We need to understand the distinctions of faith. Faith cannot alter purpose; it only acts as an agent to assist in fulfilling the predetermined purpose of God. If God's plan requires that we suffer certain opposition in order to accomplish His purpose, then faith becomes the vehicle that enables us to persevere and delivers us through the test.

On the other hand, the enemy afflicts the believer in an attempt to abort the purpose of God. Faith is a night watchman sent to guard the purpose of God. It will deliver us out of the hand of the enemy—the enemy being anyone or anything that hinders the purpose of God in our lives.

Hebrews 11 discusses at length the definition of faith. It shares the deeds of faith in verses 32-35 and finally discusses the perseverance of faith in verses 35-39. There are distinctions of faith as well. In Hebrews 11:32-35, the teaching has placed an intensified kind of emphasis on the distinct faith that escapes peril and overcomes obstacles: *"Quenched the fury of the flames, and escaped the edge of the sword; whose weakness was turned to strength; and who became powerful in battle and routed foreign armies"* (Hebrews 11:34 NIV).

However, in the verses that end the chapter, almost as if they were footnotes, the writer deals with the distinctions of another kind of faith. In his closing remarks, he shares that there were some other believers whose faith was exemplified *through* suffering and not *from* suffering.

> *Some faced jeers and flogging, and even chains and imprisonment. They were put to death by stoning; they were sawed in two; they were killed by the sword. They went about in sheepskins and goatskins, destitute, persecuted and mistreated* (Hebrews 11:36-37 NIV).

Prayer

Almighty God, I pray for the faith of David and Joseph and all the many believers who were privileged to live during the time Jesus was on earth. May my faith in You, Your Son, and the Holy Spirit permeate my being through and through as a testament of Your reign and rule in my life. In Jesus's name, amen.

Declaration

Through my faith in God I will
gain the promises of God!

Faith to Take a Stand

It was by faith that Rahab the prostitute was not destroyed with the people in her city who refused to obey God. For she had given a friendly welcome to the spies (Hebrews 11:31 NLT).

GOD WANTS YOU to believe Him. Make a decision and stand on it. Rahab decided to take a stand on the side of God's people. She hid the spies. She made the decision based on her faith. She took action. Faith is a fact and faith is an action. She took action because she believed God would deliver her when Jericho fell to the Israelites.

Sarah received strength to carry and deliver a child when she was well past childbearing age. She took action because she judged Him faithful who had promised. *"Through faith also Sara herself received strength to conceive seed, and was delivered of a child when she was past age, because she judged him faithful who had promised"* (Hebrews 11:11 KJV). She went through the birth process and delivered a child not because of her circumstance—but because of her faith. She believed God.

God wants your faith to be developed. Regardless of your position and your past, God raises people up equally. Faith is an equal opportunity business. No matter how many mistakes you have made, it is still faith that God honors. You see, you may have blown it, but God is in the business of restoring broken lives. You may have been like Rahab, but if you can believe God, He will save your house. You know, He didn't save only her. He saved her entire household. All the other homes in Jericho were destroyed. The only house God saved in the city was the house where the prostitute lived.

You might think He would have saved some nice little lady's house. Perhaps He would have saved some cottage housing an old woman or a little widow's house, with petunias growing on the sidewalk. No, God saved the whore's house. Was it because He wanted it? No, He wanted the faith. That is what moves God.

Prayer

God, hear my prayer of remorse for the times I have not taken a stand for You, for righteousness, for forgiveness. Lord, hear my prayer of repentance as I ask You for redemption for my sins. You, Almighty, are faithful to save those who put their trust in You. May today You hear my faith in You through this prayer, my actions, and the stand I take against evil and for good. In Jesus's precious name, amen.

Declaration

I stand on the side of God and His people!

Forgetting Your Misery

You will forget your misery; it will be like water flowing away. Your life will be brighter than the noonday. Even darkness will be as bright as morning. Having hope will give you courage. You will be protected and will rest in safety. You will lie down unafraid, and many will look to you for help (Job 11:16-19 NLT).

IT IS INCONCEIVABLE to the injured that the injury can be forgotten. However, to forget isn't to develop amnesia. It is to reach a place where the misery is pulled from the memory as a stinger pulled out of an insect bite. Once the stinger is gone, healing is inevitable. This passage from Job 11 points out so eloquently that the memory is as "water flowing away." Stand in a stream with waters around your ankles. The waters that pass by you at that moment, you will never see again. So it is with the misery that has challenged your life—let it go. Let it pass away.

The brilliance of morning is in sharp contrast to the darkness of night; simply stated, it was night, but now it is day. Perhaps David understood the aftereffects of traumatic deliverance when he said, *"Weeping may endure for a night, but joy comes in the morning"* (Psalm 30:5 NKJV).

There is such security that comes when we are safe in the arms of God. When we become secure in our relationship with God, we begin to allow the past to fall from us as a garment. We remember it but choose not to wear it!

I am convinced that resting in the relationship that we have with God heals us from feelings of vulnerability. It is a shame that many Christians have not yet rested in the promise of God. Everyone needs reassurance. Little girls as well as grown women need that sense of security. In the process of creating Eve, the mother of all living, God's timing was crucial. In fact, God did not unveil her until everything she needed was provided. From establishment to relationship, all things were in order. Innately the woman tends to need stability. She wants no sudden changes that disrupt or compromise her security.

Prayer

God of the universe, with Your help, I will let my misery flow past me as river waters. I know that dwelling on negative thoughts is not healthy, so please, Lord, fill my mind and spirit with Your positive and good thoughts. I will turn to Your Word and fill my being with all the wisdom and love and joy contained there. Thank You for the Bible and for Your only Son, Jesus, and in His name I pray, amen.

Declaration

I choose to be hopeful, which will give me courage. I will be protected and rest in safety unafraid, because I look to God for help.

Friendship

*No longer do I call you servants, for a servant does
not know what his master is doing; but I have called
you friends, for all things that I heard from My Father
I have made known to you* (John 15:15 NKJV).

WHAT HAPPENS WHEN friendship takes an unusual form?
Did you know that God, our ultimate Friend, sometimes
manipulates the actions of our enemies to cause them to
work as friends in order to accomplish His will in our lives?
God can bless you through the worst of relationships! That
is why we must learn how to accept even the relationships
that seem to be painful or negative. The time, effort, and pain
we invest in them is not wasted, because *God knows how to
make adversity feed destiny into our lives!*

In short, the bleeding trail of broken hearts and wounded
relationships ultimately leads us to the richness of God's
purpose in us. Periodically each of us will hear a knock on
the door. It is the knock of our old friend Judas, whose cold
kiss and calloused heart usher us into the will of God. To be
sure, these betrayals call bloody tears to our eyes and nail us
to a cold cross. Nevertheless, the kiss of betrayal can never
abort the precious promises of God in our life! The challenge
is to sit at the table with Judas on one side and John on the
other—and to treat one no differently from the other, even
though we are distinctly aware of each one's identity and
agenda.

If you have been betrayed or wounded by someone you brought too close, please forgive them. They really were a blessing. You will only be better when you cease to be bitter! I cannot stop your hurts from coming; neither can I promise that everyone who sits at the table with you is loyal. But I can suggest that the sufferings of success give us direction and build character within us.

Finally, as you find the grace to reevaluate your enemies and realize that many of them were friends in disguise, I can only place a warm hand of solace on your sobbing shoulder and wipe the gentle rain of soft tears from your eyes. As God heals what hurt you have, I want to whisper in your ears, "Betrayal is only sweetened when it is accompanied by survival. Live on, my friend, live on!"

Prayer

Heavenly Father, thank You for Your friendship. That You would call me Your friend is most humbling, and I will strive to be Your BFF. People have not lived up to my expectations of what a friend should be, but I trust that You will use those experiences for my benefit. Give me Your perspective, Lord, about friends and how You want me to relate to them. Thank You. In the name of Jesus, amen.

Declaration

I will cease to be bitter so I can be better!

A New Body

Don't you realize that all of you together are the temple of God and that the Spirit of God lives in you? God will destroy anyone who destroys this temple. For God's temple is holy, and you are that temple (1 Corinthians 3:16-17 NLT).

MOST OF US COME TO the Lord damaged. We're dead spiritually, damaged emotionally, and decaying physically. When He saved you, He made alive your dead spirit. He also promised you a new body. Then He began the massive renovation necessary to repair your damaged thoughts about life, about others, and about yourself—here come all types of nails, saws, levels, bricks, and blocks.

While we dress and smell nice outwardly, people do not hear the constant hammering and sawing going on inwardly as the Lord works within us, trying desperately to meet a deadline and present us as a newly constructed masterpiece fit for the Master's use.

> *For we are his workmanship, created in Christ Jesus unto good works, which God hath before ordained that we should walk in them* (Ephesians 2:10 KJV).

Beneath our pasted smiles and pleasant greetings, we alone hear the rumblings of the midnight shift. God is constantly excommunicating lethal thoughts that hinder us from grasping the many-faceted callings and giftings buried beneath the rubble of our minds.

No matter who we meet, once we get to know them, we begin to realize that they have their own challenges. Have you ever met someone and thought they had it all together? Once you become closely involved with someone, you will begin to notice a twisted board here, a loose nail there, or even a squeaky frame!

Yes, we all need the Lord to help us with ourselves. We came to Him as condemned buildings, and He reopened the places that satan thought would never be inhabited. The Holy Spirit moved in, but He brought His hammers and His saw with Him.

Prayer

Master Builder, feel free to bring Your hammer and nails and go to work on me whenever and wherever You see broken pieces. I completely trust Your building skills and know that I will be a better person—ready to give You all the glory for making me a better person! Thank You, Father, and it is in Your Son's name I pray, amen.

Declaration

The Lord dwells within me—I am a newly built model ready to serve!

Growth

*The Lord has made everything for his own purposes,
even the wicked for a day of disaster* (Proverbs 16:4 NLT).

GREAT GROWTH DOESN'T come into your life through mountaintop experiences. Great growth comes through the valleys and low places where you feel limited and vulnerable. The time God is really moving in your life may seem to be the lowest moment you have ever experienced.

> *Look, I go forward, but He is not there, and backward, but I cannot perceive Him; when He works on the left hand, I cannot behold Him; when He turns to the right hand, I cannot see Him* (Job 23:8-9 NKJV).

God is working on you, your faith, and your character when the blessing is delayed. The blessing is the reward that comes after you learn obedience through the things you suffered while waiting for it! I am not finished with the left hand—nor do I want to be finished. The prerequisite of the mountain is the valley.

If there is no valley, there is no mountain. After you've been through this process a few times, you begin to realize that the valley is only a sign that with a few more steps, you'll be at the mountain again! Thus if the left hand is where He works (and it is), if the left hand is where He teaches us (and it is), then at the end of every class is a promotion. So just hold on!

It is difficult to perceive God's workings on the left hand. God makes definite moves on the right hand, but when He works on the left, you may think He has forgotten you! If you've been living on the left side, you've been through a period that didn't seem to have the slightest stirring. It seemed as if everything you wanted to see God move upon stayed still.

"Has He gone on vacation? Has He forgotten His promise?" you've asked. The answer is no! God hasn't forgotten. You simply need to understand that sometimes He moves openly. I call them right-hand blessings. But sometimes He moves silently, tiptoeing around in the invisible, working in the shadows. You can't see Him, for He is working on the left side.

Prayer

Dear God, sometimes I am confused and wonder where You are. Yet I know deep down You are always with me. I have the confidence and the peace that passes my understanding. So, when troubles come and I can't feel Your presence, I will remember that You are working on me behind the scenes—left and right—and You make everything for Your purpose. I trust You and praise You for who You are—the great I AM. In Jesus's name, amen.

Declaration

I'm growing spiritually because I read God's Word daily and listen for His teachings.

Glory to Glory

*But **we all**, with unveiled face, beholding as in a mirror the glory of the Lord, **are being transformed** into the same image from glory to glory, just as by the Spirit of the Lord* (2 Corinthians 3:18 NKJV).

I'VE LEARNED TO BE thankful for the end results. Through every test and trial you must tell yourself what Job said: "I shall come forth as pure gold. I might not come forth today. It might not even be tomorrow. But when God gets through melting out all the impurities and scraping off the dross, when the boiling and the toilings of trouble have receded and the liquefied substances in my life have become stable and fixed, then I will shine!" (See Job 23:10.)

You bubbling, tempestuous saint who is enduring a time of walking through the left side of God, be strong and very courageous. The process always precedes the promise! Soon you will be reshaped and remade into a gold chalice from which only the King can drink. All dross is discarded; all fear is removed.

The spectators will gather to ask how such a wonderful vessel was made out of such poor materials. They will behold the jewels of your testimony and the brilliant glory of that fresh anointing. Some will wonder if you are the same person that they used to know. How do you answer? Simply stated, just say no!

Now you sit on the Master's right side, ready and available to be used, a vessel of honor unto Him. No matter how glorious it is to sit on His right hand and be brought to a position of power, just remember that although you have overcome now, you were boiled down and hollowed out while you lived on the left side of God. Join me in looking back over your life.

Review your left-side experiences. Taste the bitter tears and the cold winds of human indifference, and never, ever let anyone make you forget. You and I know. It's our secret, whether we tell them or sit quietly and make small talk. You've not always been where you are or shined as you shine. What can I say? You've come a long way, baby!

Prayer

Oh yes, Lord, You brought me out of the mess I made of my life the moment I accepted You as my Lord and Savior! Thank You! And, Lord, I'm looking forward to what You have for me next—what troubles and toiling You will bring me through that will make me fit more perfectly for the Kingdom work You have for me.

Declaration

It is a privilege and an honor to share my testimony of being transformed from glory to glory by the Spirit of the Lord!

Resilience

Brothers and sisters, I do not consider myself yet to have taken hold of it. But one thing I do: Forgetting what is behind and straining toward what is ahead, I press on toward the goal to win the prize for which God has called me heavenward in Christ Jesus (Philippians 3:13-14 NIV).

ALTHOUGH HEROES DON'T have to be perfect, I realize they must be people who are resilient enough to survive tragedy and adversity. All of us have experienced the pain of adversity in our warfare, whether it was a physical, emotional, economical, spiritual, or sexual attack. Regardless which category the attack falls under, all of them are very personal in nature.

Real heroes not only survive the incident, but they also overcome the lingering side effects that can come from it. Why do I say that? If you don't survive, you can't save anyone. No young man in a combat zone can carry his wounded comrade if he himself does not survive. Live long enough to invest the wealth of your experience in the release of some other victim whom satan desires to bind or incapacitate!

> *And truly, if they had been mindful of that country from whence they came out, they might have had opportunity to have returned* (Hebrews 11:15 KJV).

The faith of these heroes in Hebrews 11 sets them apart from others. Your convictions cause you to be distinctly different from others whose complacency you can't seem to share. The people referred to in Hebrews 11 were not mindful of where they came from. In other words, their minds were full of where they were going. These valiant heroes were not perfect, but they were convinced that *what God had promised He was able to perform.* Now if their minds had been full of their origin instead of their destiny, they would have gone back.

Be assured that people always move in the direction of their mind. Whatever your mind is full of, that is where you eventually move. Thank God for people who can see the invisible—and *touch with their faith the intangible promises of God.*

Prayer

My Hero, God Almighty, I come before You with a thankful and humbled heart. May I always look to You for direction to move forward toward the destiny You wrote for me before I was even conceived in my mother's womb. I know You are able and willing to keep the promises made to all Your children who love You. Glory to You, my Hero, my Savior. Amen!

Declaration

I will strive to be a survivor for Christ—moving forward through every battle to win the prize!

Fruitfulness

As apostles of Christ we certainly had a right to make some demands of you, but instead we were like children among you. Or we were like a mother feeding and caring for her own children. We loved you so much that we shared with you not only God's Good News but our own lives, too (1 Thessalonians 2:7-8 NLT).

SATAN WANTS TO USE you as a legal entry into this world or into your family. That's how he destroyed the human race with the first family. He knows that you are the entrance of all things. You are the doors of life. Be careful what you let come through you. Close the doors to the planting of the enemy. Then know that when travail comes into your spirit, it's because you're going to give birth.

You will give birth! That's why you have suffered pain. Your spirit is signaling you that something is trying to get through. Don't become so preoccupied with the pain that you forget to push the baby. Sometimes you're pushing the pain and not the baby, and you're so engrossed with what's hurting you that you're not doing what it takes to produce fruit in your life.

When you see sorrow multiply, it is a sign that God is getting ready to send something to you. Don't settle for the pain and not get the benefit. Hold out. Disregard the pain and get the promise. Understand that God has promised some things to you that He wants you to have, and you've got to stay there on the table until you get to the place where you ought to be in the Lord.

After all, the pain is forgotten when the baby is born. What is the pain when compared with the baby? Some may have dropped the baby. That happens when you become so engrossed with the pain that you leave the reward behind you. Your attention gets focused on the wrong thing. You can be so preoccupied with how bad it hurts that you miss the joy of a vision giving birth.

Prayer

Word of Life, shower me with Your vision. Show me how I fit into Your Kingdom here on earth so I can make a positive difference. Make Your vision my vision. Give me the strength and wisdom to follow through with the plans You have for me—plans to prosper me and not to harm me, to give me hope and a future, as Jeremiah 29:11 declares. Use me as You please. In Jesus's name, amen.

Declaration

Here I am, Lord. Use me for Your glory!

Overcoming Pain

Love never gives up, never loses faith, is always hopeful, and endures through every circumstance (1 Corinthians 13:7 NLT).

IN THE DELIVERY ROOM, the midwife tells a woman, "Push." The baby will not come forth if the mother doesn't push. God will not allow you to become trapped in a situation without escape. But you have to push while you are in pain if you intend to produce. I'm told that when the pain is at its height, that's when they instruct you to push, not when the pain recedes. When the pain is at its ultimate expression, that is the time you need to push.

As you begin to push in spite of the pain, the pain recedes into the background because you become preoccupied with the change rather than the problem. Push! You don't have time to cry. Push! You don't have time to be suicidal. Push! This is not the time to give up. Push—because God is about to birth a promise through you. Cry if you must, and groan if you have to, but keep on pushing because God has promised that if it is to come into the world, it has to pass through you.

There remains a conflict between past pain and future desire. Here is the conflict. He said, *"In pain you shall bring forth children; your desire shall be for your husband, and he shall rule over you"* (Genesis 3:16 NKJV). In other words, you have so much pain in producing the child that, if you don't have balance between past pain and future desire, you will quit producing. God says, "After the pain, your desire shall be for your husband." Pain is swallowed by desire.

Impregnated with destiny, women and men of promise must bear down in the spirit. The past hurts; the pain is genuine. However, you must learn to get in touch with something other than your pain. If you do not have desire, you won't have the tenacity to resurrect. Desire will come back. After the pain is over, desire follows, because it takes desire to be productive again.

Prayer

Dear Father, in Jesus's name I come to You in pain. Please give me the desire to get past the pain and birth what You have for me to bring forth. I want to be productive for You, Lord. I realize I have a God-given destiny, and I want to accomplish all that You have designed for me. I will give You all the praise and glory for all that I push out!

Declaration

**I will push through the pain
and focus on the future!**

Desires of Your Heart

Delight yourself also in the Lord, and He shall give you the desires of your heart (Psalm 37:4 NKJV).

ABRAHAM HAD MANY promises from God regarding his descendants. God told Abraham that his seed would be as the sands of the sea and the stars of Heaven.

> *That in blessing I will bless thee, and in multiplying I will multiply thy seed as the stars of the heaven, and as the sand which is upon the sea shore; and thy seed shall possess the gate of his enemies* (Genesis 22:17 KJV).

There were two promises of seed given to Abraham. God said his seed would be as the sands of the earth. That promise represents the natural, physical nation of Israel. These were the people of the Old Covenant.

However, God didn't stop there. He also promised that Abraham's seed would be as the stars of Heaven. These are the people of the New Covenant, the exalted people. That's the Church. We are exalted in Christ Jesus. We, too, are seed of Abraham. We are the stars of Heaven.

God had more plans for Abraham's descendants than to simply start a new nation on earth. He planned a new spiritual Kingdom that will last forever. The plan started as a seed, but it ended up as stars.

The only thing between the seed and the stars was the woman. Can you see why Sarah herself had to receive strength to conceive a seed when she was past childbearing age? Because the old man gave her a seed, she gave him the stars of Heaven. Whatever God gives you, He wants it to be multiplied in the womb of your spirit. When you bring it forth, it shall be greater than the former.

Prayer

Father in Heaven and in my heart, thank You for the promises You have given all who believe. Those in the Old Testament and those in the New are recipients of Your promise to give us the desires of our hearts. Lord God, the desire of my heart is to worship and praise You every day into eternity. Create in me the desire to fulfill Your will in my life. In Jesus's name, amen.

Declaration

The desire of my heart is to fulfill the will of God in my life!

Blessings

And all these blessings shall come upon you and overtake you, because you obey the voice of the Lord your God (Deuteronomy 28:2 NKJV).

EVERY ASPECT OF CREATION that receives anything gives it back to God. The mineral kingdom gives strength to the vegetable kingdom. The vegetable kingdom is consumed by the animal kingdom. Everything reaches the point of return.

Near my home, crouched in the valley beneath the proud, swelling mountains of West Virginia, runs a river whose rushing waters cannot be contained. The Elk River cannot keep receiving the cascading streams of water from the ground in the mountains without finally pushing its blessing on into the Kanawha River. This river, though larger, is no less able to break the laws of the kingdom. It drinks in the waters from its sources and then turns its attention to its destiny and gives back its waters to the system. So the mighty Ohio River says amen.

From the Ohio to the Mississippi and on into the Gulf of Mexico, each body of water receives only to give. You see, my friend, success is not success without a successor.

We as Christians reach fulfillment when we come to the point where we bring to the Lord all that we have and worship Him on the other side of accomplishment. This need to return an answer to the Sender is as instinctive as answering a ringing phone. There is a ringing in the heart of a believer that requires an answer.

Why do we answer a phone? We do so because of our insatiable curiosity to know who is calling. God is calling us. His ring has sounded through our triumphs and conquests. A deep sound in the recesses of a heart turned toward God suggests that there is a deeper relationship on the other side of the blessing.

As wonderful as it is to be blessed with promises, there is still a faint ringing that suggests the Blesser is better than the blessing. It is a ringing that many people overlook. The noise of the bustling, blaring sound of survival can be deafening. There must be a degree of spirituality in order to hear and respond to the inner ringing of the call of God!

Prayer

Dear Blesser, I have so, so many blessings to thank You for—from my family and friends to the birds and the trees, to the most generous Blessing and Gift of all: Your Son, Jesus Christ. You are the all-time best Blesser, and I am so very grateful. May your blessings multiply from one to another worldwide, Lord, and may I pass along to others Your abundant provisions.

Declaration

**God's blessings will overtake me because
I obey the voice of the Lord my God.**

Time

Now it happened on the third day that Esther put on her royal robes and stood in the inner court of the king's palace, across from the king's house, while the king sat on his royal throne in the royal house, facing the entrance of the house. So it was, when the king saw Queen Esther standing in the court, that she found favor in his sight, and the king held out to Esther the golden scepter that was in his hand. Then Esther went near and touched the top of the scepter (Esther 5:1-2 NKJV).

ESTHER'S CHANGING HER APPAREL signifies our need to alter our circumstances to facilitate the success of the vision that is before us. Everything must be committed to the goal—body, soul, and spirit. When the king beheld a prepared person, he granted an expected end. He drew her into his presence because she had prepared herself for her time. Please hear me; there is a blessing on the horizon for the person of purpose. Only the prepared will be eligible to receive this endowment from the Lord, so be ready!

Like sands cascading down in an hourglass, time silently slips away, without the chance of retrieval, from almost everyone every day. The misuse of anything as precious as time should be a crime. If someone steals your car, it would be an inconvenience but not a tragedy, because you can easily acquire another. If someone snatches your wallet, it would be an annoyance, but a few phone calls would salvage the majority of your losses. But who can you call if you suffer the loss of time? And not just time in general, but *your* time? Who can afford to miss their time? I can't. Can you?

Ask God to give you the patience you need to become empowered to perform. You may feel like a child waiting in line at a carnival. There will always be times when other people receive their dues, and you are forced to wait your turn. This is not injustice; it is order. There is nothing unjust about order. But after I have waited my turn and paid my dues, there comes a time when it is all mine. The most frightening thing I can think of is the possibility of missing my time.

Generally, somewhere on the other side of a tremendous test is the harvest of your dream. If you have planted the seeds of a promise and watered them thoroughly with the tears of struggle, then this is your time. Woe unto the person who has seeds without water. The tears of struggle become the irrigation of the Holy Spirit. It is through your own tear-filled struggles that God directs the waters of life to the field of your dreams.

Prayer

Lord God, I enter Your presence with praise and worship for who You are—the Creator God who was and is and is to come. Before time You existed, and You will live forevermore. That is mind-boggling to me. So I pray that You will teach me how to use wisely the time You give me. That I won't waste time on frivolous wants and unimportant endeavors. Your timing is perfect, and the sooner I submit to Your timing, the sooner I will accomplish my purpose. In Jesus's name I pray, amen.

Declaration

I will be prepared and ready to receive the endowment of time from the Lord!

Harvest

Those who plant in tears will harvest with shouts of joy (Psalm 126:5 NLT).

GREATNESS HAS A TREMENDOUS THIRST. This thirst is quenched in the tear-stained struggle toward destiny. One thing I learned about life is neither fellowship nor friendship can lower the price of personal sacrifice. What I mean is, no one can water your dreams but you. No matter how many people hold your hand, you still must shed your own tears. Others can cry with you, but they can't cry for you! That's the bad news. The good news is there will be a harvest at the end of your tears!

On the other hand, you must know when you have shed enough tears. It is important that you don't get stuck in a state of lamentation. In short, don't overwater the promise!

A certain number of tears are necessary during the time of sowing. But when you have come into harvest, don't let the devil keep you weeping. Tears are for the sower, but joy is for the harvester. Harvest your field with joy. You've paid your dues and shed your tears—now reap your benefits. It's your turn. Reap in knee-slapping, teeth-baring, hand-clapping, foot-stomping joy!

They weep as they go to plant their seed, but they sing as they return with the harvest (Psalm 126:6 NLT).

Everything has a season and a purpose (see Ecclesiastes 3:1). You need to understand that God is just and that He appropriates opportunities to advance according to His purpose. I don't know whether this is true for everyone, but usually obscurity precedes notoriety.

The first Psalm teaches that the blessed person meditates on the Word while waiting. It says that you bring forth fruit in your own season. It is good to recognize your season and prepare for it before it comes. But the fruit will not grow prior to its right season. Don't demand fruit when it is not in season. Even restaurant menus have a notation that says certain items can be served only when their fruit is in season.

Prayer

God Most High, You know that I have shed tears and wept from time to time over the years. You also know that I have experienced fruitful seasons as well as dry seasons. I stand on Your promise that the harvest from those tears and weeping will come with joyful shouts and singing! Thank You for balancing the ups and downs of life— You are always faithful. You are my Rock and my salvation. In Jesus's name, amen.

Declaration

The God of the harvest is my Redeemer!

All Good Things

For the Lord God is our sun and our shield. He gives us grace and glory. The Lord will withhold no good thing from those who do what is right (Psalm 84:11 NLT).

WHAT GOOD IS HAVING your season if, over your head, gather the gloomy clouds of warning that keep thundering a nagging threat in your ears?

First, let me rebuke the spirit of fear. Fear will hide in the closet as we are blessed and make strange noises when no one else is around. We need to declare God to this fear. We dare not fall in love with what God is doing, but we must always be in love with who God is. God does not change. That's why we must set our affections on things that are eternal. He says, *"For I am the Lord, I do not change"* (Malachi 3:6 NKJV).

It is such a comfort, when the chilly voice of fear speaks, to know that God doesn't change. His purpose doesn't change. His methods may change, but His ultimate purpose doesn't. People have a need to know what comes next. God doesn't always make us privy to such information, but *He has promised that if we walk uprightly, He will not withhold any good thing from us* (see Psalm 84:11). I therefore conclude that if God withheld it, then it was no longer working for my good. I am then ready for the next assignment—it will be good for me.

What we must always remember is God can bless us in many different areas. Even while we were in the waiting periods of our lives, some other area was being blessed. There are really no "down" times in God. We only feel down when, like spoiled children, we demand that He continue to give us what He did at one stage without appreciating the fact that we are moving from one stage to another. It is what the Word calls going from faith to faith (see Romans 1:17).

God has put too much training into you to leave you without any area of productivity. He has been grooming you in the furnace of affliction. When He begins to move you into your season, don't allow even well-meaning people to intimidate you with the fear of change.

Prayer

Dear God of blessings, abundance, and provision, I praise and worship You for all the many good things You have given me. You know my heart, so You know how hard I try to do what is right— but many times I fail. Thank You for forgiving me when I repent of my failure. Leaning on You for everything is my intent and longing. Please be patient with me, Lord. In Jesus's name, amen.

Declaration

My God gives me grace and glory and every good thing when I do what is right.

Victory

But thanks be to God, who gives us the victory through our Lord Jesus Christ (1 Corinthians 15:57 NKJV).

THE OBSCURE SIDE OF a struggle is the awesome wrestling match many people have with success. First, success is given only at the end of great struggle. If it were easy, anybody could do it. Success is success only because it relates to struggle. How can you have victory without conflict? To receive something without struggle lessens its personal value.

Success is the reward that God gives to the diligent who, through perseverance, obtain the promise. There is no way to receive what God has for your life without fighting the obstacles and challenges that block your way to conquest. In fact, people who procrastinate do so because they are desperately trying to find a way to reach the goal without going through the struggle.

When I was a youngster, we kids used to go into the stores and change the price tags on the items we could not afford. We weren't stealing, we thought, because we did pay something. It just wasn't nearly what the vendor wanted us to pay. I guess we thought we would put the product on sale without the permission of the store manager.

I believe many people are trying to do the same thing today in their spiritual lives. They are attempting to get a discount on the promises of God. That doesn't work in the Kingdom. Whatever it costs, it costs; there is no swapping the price tags. You must pay your own way. Your payment helps you to appreciate the blessings when they come because you know the expense. You will not easily jeopardize the welfare of something not easily attained.

The zeal it takes to be effective at accomplishing a goal ushers you up the steps of life. As you journey up the steps, it becomes increasingly difficult to be successful without others finding you offensive. Some people will find your success offensive, whether or not you are arrogant. They are offended at what God does for you.

Prayer

Heavenly Father, as I struggle to attain success, may I continuously remember that there is a cost for the reward. Paying that cost will help me appreciate the blessings when they come, because I know that I paid the price honestly. Help me to endure what others may have to say about my God-given success, and give me the fortitude to push through the challenges, knowing that on the other side is the kind of success You offer, which is always the best. In Jesus's name, amen.

Declaration

Success is the promised victory God gives me when I am diligent and persevere through every struggle along the way.

Whatsoevers

Hear my prayer, O Lord! Listen to my cries for help! Don't ignore my tears. For I am your guest—a traveler passing through, as my ancestors were before me (Psalm 39:12 NLT).

NOW UNDERSTAND THAT nothing fuels prayer like need. Neither the tranquil mood of a calming organ nor a dimly lit room with hallowed walls can promote the power of prayer like the aching of a heart that says, "I need Thee every hour." The presence of need will produce the power of prayer. Even the agnostic will make a feeble attempt at prayer in the crisis of a moment. The alcoholic who staggers toward a car he knows he shouldn't drive will, before the night is over, find himself attempting to dial the number of Heaven and sputter in slurred speech a fleeting prayer in the presence of near-mishap and malady.

Prayer is our confession, "I don't have it all." Prayer is our admitting to ourselves that, in spite of the architectural designs and scientific accomplishments, we need a higher power. Prayer is the humbling experience of the most arrogant mind confessing, "There are still some things I cannot resolve."

The presence of prayer is, in itself, the birthplace of praise. Prayer is our acknowledging the sovereign authority of *the God who can!* You ask, "Can what?" God can do whatever He wants to do, whenever He wants to do it. What a subliminal solace to know the sovereignty of God!

Each of us must have the curiosity and the inner thirst to move beyond our images into our realities. It is difficult, sometimes even painful, to face the truth about our circumstances and then possess the courage to ask for God's best for our lives. If prayer is to be meaningful, it cannot be fictitious. It must be born out of the pantings of a heart that can admit its need. If we refrain from airing our particular dilemmas with anyone else, at least we must be honest enough to come before God with an open heart and a willing mind to receive the "whatsoevers" that He promised to the "whosoevers" in His Word!

But I know, that even now, whatsoever thou wilt ask of God, God will give it thee (John 11:22 KJV).

Prayer

Lord, may this prayer that I offer to You in the holy name of Christ Jesus be truthful and straight from my heart. It is my sincere pleasure to give You all the honor and glory that You deserve. I offer You my open heart and willing mind to accept whatsoever You have in store for me—be it a dilemma or discipline, riches or remnants. Father, thank You for loving me, a whosoever who loves You too.

Declaration

I stand strong on the fact that I can go directly to God in prayer in every circumstance and situation!

From One to Another

I know all the things you do, that you are neither hot nor cold. I wish that you were one or the other! But since you are like lukewarm water, neither hot nor cold, I will spit you out of my mouth! (Revelation 3:15-16 NLT)

I LOVE TO SURROUND MYSELF with people who can stir up the fire in me. Some people in the body of Christ know just what to say to ignite the very fire in you. However, no one can ignite in you what you don't possess! If the cold winds of opposition have banked the fire and your dream is dying down, I challenge you to rekindle your desire to achieve whatever God has called you to do. Don't lose your fire. You need that continued spark for excellence to overcome all the blight of being ostracized.

Fire manifests itself in two ways. First, it gives light. Second, fire gives heat. Every man and woman of God must also remember that fire needs fuel. Feed the fire. Feed it with the words of people who motivate you. Feed it with vision and purpose. When stress comes, fan the flames. Gather the wood. Pour gasoline if you have to, but don't let it die!

Sometimes just seeing God bless someone else gives you the fortitude to put a demand on the promise that God has given you. I don't mean envy but a strong provocation to receive. Look at the situation of Hannah, Elkanah's wife, in 1 Samuel 1. She wanted to have a child. In order to stir up Hannah, God used a girl named Peninnah who was married to the same man but able to bear children. The more Hannah saw Peninnah have children, the more she desired her own. Peninnah provoked Hannah; she stirred Hannah's embers. She made Hannah pray. It wasn't that Hannah got jealous and didn't want to see Peninnah be blessed. She didn't begrudge the other woman her blessing. She just wanted her own.

If seeing others blessed makes you want to sabotage their success, then you will not be fruitful. I have learned how to rejoice over the blessings of others and realize that the same God who blessed them can bless me also. Other people's blessings ought to challenge you to see that it can be done.

Prayer

Oh God of blessings, abundance, and provision, may I humble myself to see that You don't favor one over another—You love all people the same. That is hard for me to understand, but I know it's true. You are just and righteous to all. Lord, remove every trace of jealousy from me so I can see others as You see them—members of Your family, my kinfolk. This I ask in Jesus's name, amen.

Declaration

To love and rejoice over the blessings of others is my goal, because it is God's way and will.

The Blood of Jesus

But if we are living in the light, as God is in the light, then we have fellowship with each other, and the blood of Jesus, his Son, cleanses us from all sin (1 John 1:7 NLT).

THE BLOOD IS THE ONLY element in the body that reaches, affects, and fuels all other parts of the body. This rich, reddish-purple elixir flows silently through the cardiovascular system like high-powered cars moving on interstate highways. It carries the cargo of much-needed oxygen molecules and nutrients that are necessary to sustain life in every cell of the body.

If the blood is restricted long enough from any member of the body, that member will internally asphyxiate and begin to change colors. Its asphyxiated cells can quickly die—even without an external assailant—for their affliction is the result of internal deprivation.

Every member, every limb and organ in the human body, needs the blood. Along with its culinary duty of delivering soluble dietary contents throughout the body, our blood has the additional responsibility of functioning as a paramedic. Its white blood cells stand ready to attack adverse intruders in the form of bacteria or foreign cells or any other foreign substance that may try to disrupt the vitality of the body. The white blood cells are the body's "militia." These cells are uniquely equipped to fight off attacking bacteria and expel them from the body—stripping them of their power and robbing them of their spoils.

> *Just as our bodies have many parts and each part has a special function, so it is with Christ's body. We are many parts of one body, and we all belong to each other* (Romans 12:4-5 NLT).

The physical body echoes and illustrates the power of the blood in the Church, the mystical body of Christ. Every member of the body of Christ—regardless of morality, maturity, or position—needs the life-giving blood of Jesus. Without the blood, we cease to have the proof of our kinship. Isn't the blood what physicians test to determine and verify who is the father of a child? Without the blood, we are only bastard children camouflaged as real heirs. Without His blood, we are pseudo-heirs trying to receive the promises reserved for the legitimate sons and daughters of God!

Prayer

My prayer today to You, my Lord and Savior, is a song called "Nothing But the Blood" that expresses my heart and my spirit: "What can wash away my sin? What can make me whole again? Nothing but the blood of Jesus! Oh, precious is the flow that makes me white as snow. Nothing can for sin atone, naught of good that I have done. This is all my hope and peace, this is all my righteousness—nothing but the blood of Jesus!" And it is in His name I come to You, God. Amen.

Declaration

Because I am living in the Light of God and
washed clean by the blood of Jesus, I have
genuine fellowship with other believers.

Eternal Inheritance

God the Father knew you and chose you long ago, and his Spirit has made you holy. As a result, you have obeyed him and have been cleansed by the blood of Jesus Christ. May God give you more and more grace and peace (1 Peter 1:2 NLT).

WE DID NOT NEED the blood only for when we cried out to the Lord to come into our hearts by faith and rescue us from impending danger. On the contrary, we still need that same blood today. All our strength and nourishment and every promise and miracle must flow to us through the blood. Satan hates the blood—not only because it redeemed us but also because it continues to give us life from day to day!

*Just think how much more the blood of Christ will purify our consciences from sinful deeds so that we can worship the living God. For by the power of the eternal Spirit, Christ offered himself to God as a perfect sacrifice for our sins. That is why he is the one who mediates a new covenant between God and people, so that all who are called can **receive the eternal inheritance God has promised them**. For Christ died to set them free from the penalty of the sins they had committed under that first covenant* (Hebrews 9:14-15 NLT).

We have lost our teaching of the blood in this age of Pentecostalism (of which I am adamantly a part). We have learned about the Spirit of God, but we failed to teach believers about the blood. Consequently, we have produced a generation of believers who are empowered by the Spirit but do not feel forgiven! They are empowered, yet they are insecure. They are operating in the gifts but living in guilt!

Oh, hear me today! The blood must be preached. Without it we have no life. No, the preaching of the blood will not weaken the Church! To the contrary, it will relieve us of a prepaid debt. Why are we wasting the power of God on the problems of our past? The blood has already totally destroyed the past bondages that held us down! It was through the eternal Spirit of God that Jesus was able to offer up His blood. The Spirit always refers us back to the blood. There can be no Pentecost where there is no Passover!

Prayer

Thank You for the blood of Jesus that covers my sins and provides my strength and nourishment. Thank You that every promise and miracle I've received flowed to me through His blood and continues to give me life. To You, Lord God, I give all praise and glory—I worship You with every drop of blood in my body. Thank You for sharing Your one and only Son with the world, and in His name I pray, amen.

Declaration

I will never forget the sacrifice Jesus
made when He shed His blood for me.

Provision

*For if, by the trespass of the one man, death reigned
through that one man, how much more will those
who **receive God's abundant provision** of grace
and of the gift of righteousness reign in life through
the one man, Jesus Christ!* (Romans 5:17 NIV).

BEFORE ADAM COULD RECEIVE the covering God had provided, he had to disrobe himself of what he had contrived. In this process many believers are trapped. Adam stripped himself before a holy God, admitted his tragic sins, and still maintained his position as a son in the presence of God. Adam and Eve realized at that moment that the only solution for their sin was in the perfect provision of their loving God. That same loving God now reaches out to us as we are and refashions us into what we should become!

Adam stood as I do, in the warm skins of a freshly slain sacrifice that made it possible for him to continue to live. It was actually no more Adam who lived; rather, he was now living the life of the innocent lamb. Just as surely as the innocent lamb had taken Adam's place in death, Adam continued to live on, wrapped in the coverings of the lamb's life! Can you understand more clearly what Paul means when he says "accepted in the Beloved"? (See Ephesians 1:6 NKJV.) If Adam were seen out from under the covering of those bloody skins, he could not be accepted. But because of the shedding of innocent blood, there was remission of sin for him!

We hear no further mention of blame or guilt concerning the first family as they walked away from the worst moment in the history of humanity. Why? They were wrapped and protected in the provision of God. We can find no more arguments, fault-finding, or condemnation in Scripture. I have not read where Adam blamed Eve anymore. Neither did Eve judge Adam, for they both realized that had it not been for the blood, neither would have been there.

We, too, need to have this knowledge—regardless of the differences in our specific flaws, regardless of whom we would want to blame or belittle. If the blood had failed to reach the liar, then he would be as lost as the child molester! The symptoms are different, but the disease and its prognosis are the same. The disease is sin, the wage or prognosis is death, and the antidote prescribed is the blood and the blood alone. Never forget the blood, for without it we have no Good News at all!

Prayer

Father in Heaven, because of the blood of Jesus I am wrapped and protected in Your provision. I will refrain from arguing, fault-finding, or condemning others, for I realize that had it not been for the blood of Jesus, I would be as lost as those who don't know Him. Shower me with the boldness of Jesus's disciples to share the Good News with everyone I meet and those who are influenced by my life. In Jesus's name, amen.

Declaration

I choose this day to be a good, even excellent,
example of God's mercy and grace.

Possible Impossibilities

Lord, how many are my foes! How many rise up against me! Many are saying of me, "God will not deliver him." But you, Lord, are a shield around me, my glory, the One who lifts my head high. I call out to the Lord, and he answers me from his holy mountain (Psalm 3:1-4 NIV).

DAVID DECLARES THAT it is the Lord who sustains you in the perilous times of inner struggle and warfare. It is the precious peace of God that eases your tension when you are trying to make decisions in the face of criticism and cynicism. When you realize that some people do not want you to be successful, the pressure mounts drastically. Many have said, "God will not deliver him." However, many saying it still doesn't make it true.

I believe that the safest place in the whole world is in the will of God. If you align your plan with His purpose, success is imminent! On the other hand, if I have not been as successful as I would like to be, then seeking the purpose of God inevitably enriches my resources and makes the impossible attainable.

I remember when my wife and I were raising two children (now we have four). Times were tough and money was scarce. I am not the kind of husband who doesn't care about the provisions of the Lord in his house. So many were the nights that I languished over the needs in our home. Tossing and turning, praying and worrying—I wasn't sure we were going to survive the struggle.

During these times, satan always shows you images of yourself and your children wrapped up in dirty quilts, nestled under a bridge with a burning 55-gallon drum as the only source of heat. He is such a sadist. I was nearly frazzled with stress trying to raise the standard of our living. I prayed—or, more accurately, I complained to God. I explained to Him how I was living closer to Him than I had ever lived, and yet we were suffering with utility bills and lack of groceries.

I wondered, *Where are You, Lord!* I was a preacher and a pastor. All the other men of God seemed to have abundance, yet I was in need. But I knew that if the storm comes and I am in the will of God, then little else matters.

Prayer

Lord, I look to You to sustain me in times of inner struggle and warfare. Your peace eases my tension when I'm making decisions while facing criticism and cynicism. When I align my plan with Your purpose, Father, success is imminent! That's why I will seek the purpose You have designed especially for me, which will inevitably enrich my resources and make the impossible attainable. Thank You, Jesus. Amen.

Declaration

No matter the storms of life—I will stand strong because I am in my safe place: the will of God.

Identity

"Don't call me Naomi," she responded. "Instead, call me Mara, for the Almighty has made life very bitter for me. I went away full, but the Lord has brought me home empty. Why call me Naomi when the Lord has caused me to suffer and the Almighty has sent such tragedy upon me?" (Ruth 1:20-21 NLT)

IT IS IMPORTANT THAT we teach women to prepare for the winter. I believe age can be stressful for women in a way that it isn't for men—only because we have not historically recognized women at other stages in their lives. Equally disturbing is the fact that statisticians tell us women tend to live longer, more productive lives than their male counterparts. It is not their longevity of life that is disturbing; it is the fact that many times, because of an early death of their spouse, they have no sense of companionship.

The Bible admonishes us to minister to the widows. Little instruction is given in regard to the care of aged men. We need to invest some effort in encouraging older women. They have a need for more than just provision of natural substance. Many women spend their lives building their identity around their role rather than around their person. When the role changes, they feel somewhat displaced. Because being a good mother is a self-sacrificing job, when those demands have subsided, many women feel like Naomi. Her name meant "my joy." But after losing her children and husband, she said, "Change my name to Mara." Mara means "bitterness."

Don't allow changing times to change who you are. It is dangerous to lose your identity in your circumstances. Circumstances change, and when they do, the older woman can feel empty and unfulfilled. In spite of Naomi's bout with depression, God still had much for her to contribute. So just because the demands have changed, that doesn't mean your life is over. Redefine your purpose, gather your assets, and keep on living and giving. As long as you can maintain a sense of worth, you can resist the "Mara" mentality.

Prayer

Almighty God, when the time comes to realize a loss of a loved one, please grant me Your mercy and grace to identify as Your child rather than just someone left behind. When I have You, I have all that I need—my worth is all wrapped up in who You are, not what I am feeling at the moment. I seek You and Your Kingdom first, Lord, and all else will be gifted to me. I claim this in the name of Jesus. Amen.

Declaration

I will resist the Mara mentality and instead accept what John wrote— that I am a child of God.

Companionship

*I am not saying this because I am in need,
for I have learned to be content whatever the
circumstances* (Philippians 4:11 NIV).

BEING SINGLE AND DEVOTED to God does not mean it is wrong for you to want physical companionship. God ordained that need. While you are waiting, though, understand that God thinks He's your Husband. Be careful how you treat Him. He thinks He's your Man. That's why He does those special favors for you. God made you into a beautiful woman. He has been taking care of you, even when you didn't notice His provision. He is the source of every good thing. He keeps things running and provides for your daily care. He is the One who opened doors for you. He has been your edge, your Friend, and your Companion.

Those who are married seek to please their spouse. Unmarried people seek to please the Lord. There is a special relationship of power between God and the single believer. Paul wrote, *"Each person should remain in the situation they were in when God called them"* (1 Corinthians 7:20 NIV). In other words, the person who is single should be abiding, not wrestling, in singleness. Rather than spend all of our effort trying to change our position, we need to learn to develop the position where He has placed us. Isn't that what this means? *"I have learned, in whatsoever state I am, therewith to be content"* (Philippians 4:11 KJV). I speak peace to you today.

Maybe you haven't been living like you really should. Maybe your house hasn't been the house of prayer that it really could have been. I want you to take this opportunity and begin to sanctify your house and body. Maybe your body has been mauled and pawed by all sorts of people. I want you to sanctify your body unto the Lord and give your body as a living sacrifice to God (see Romans 12:1). If you can't keep your vow to God, you would never be able to keep your vow to a man. Give your body to God and sanctify yourself.

Prayer

Dear Husband, I realize that You are ultimately the only focus I need in my life—for You are the Giver of all good, which includes a spouse or not. May You give me the strength and peace to be content in life, whatever circumstance I am in today and all my tomorrows. In Jesus's holy name, amen.

Declaration

I find contentment in the loving embrace of my Lord and Savior, Jesus Christ.

Daily Nourishment

Our Father which art in heaven, hallowed be Thy name. Thy kingdom come, Thy will be done in earth, as it is in heaven. Give us this day our daily bread. And forgive us our debts, as we forgive our debtors. And lead us not into temptation, but deliver us from evil: For thine is the kingdom, and the power, and the glory, for ever. Amen (Matthew 6:9-13 KJV).

"THY KINGDOM COME" releases the downpour of the power of God. Praise will cause the very power of God to come down in your life. But what good is power without purpose? Thus Jesus taught the disciples, *"Thy will be done in earth, as it is in heaven."* That is a step up from power to purpose. Now the purpose of God comes down to your life. You can't have success without purpose!

"Give us this day our daily bread" deals with the provisions of Heaven coming down. This is more than a prayer; it is a divine direction. After receiving the power in your life, you come to understand the purpose. Never fear; if you know your purpose, God will release the provisions. There's nothing like provisions to give you the grace to forgive. It is easier to forgive when you discover that your enemies didn't stop the blessing from coming down. Here Jesus teaches His disciples to pray for the penitence of a forgiving heart.

"Forgive us our debts, as we forgive our debtors." Finally, Jesus taught us to seek deliverance from evil. Pray for the

problems that still exist at every stage and, better still, at every success in life! There must come in every person's life a turning point. At this stage of life, you begin to reevaluate what you call success.

God gets the glory when He can give you anything, and you can turn from all He gave you and still say from your heart, "Lord, I've found nothing as dear to me as You. My greatest treasure is the assurance of Your divine presence on my life. I am giving it all to You."

Prayer

When Jesus gave His disciples the model prayer— oh, what a blessing for millions, even billions, of people worldwide ever since He spoke those words. I can only imagine, Father, that You smile every time You hear one of Your earthly children praying it. I have learned so much about You and Your Son in Your Book—thank You for Your Word. In Jesus's name, amen.

Declaration

I hallow Your name, Father, and will do my part to bring Your Kingdom to earth as it is in Heaven.

Healing

He was wounded for our transgressions, He was bruised for our iniquities; the chastisement for our peace was upon Him, and by His stripes we are healed (Isaiah 53:5 NKJV).

Who Himself bore our sins in His own body on the tree, that we, having died to sins, might live for righteousness— by whose stripes you were healed (1 Peter 2:24 NKJV).

GRATITUDE AND DEFENSIVE PRAISE are contagious. Although the Bible doesn't specifically say so, I imagine that those who saw what was going on the day Jesus healed the infirm woman were caught up in praise as well.

> *And when Jesus saw her, he called her to him, and said unto her, Woman, thou art loosed from thine infirmity. And he laid His hands on her: and immediately she was made straight, and glorified God. ...And when he had said these things, all his adversaries were ashamed: and all the people rejoiced for all the glorious things that were done by him* (Luke 13:12-13, 17 KJV).

The Church also must find room to join in praise when the broken are healed. Those who missed the great blessing that day were those who decided to argue about religion. The

Bible describes Heaven as a place where the angels rejoice over one sinner who comes into the faith.

> *Likewise, I say to you, there is joy in the presence of the angels of God over one sinner who repents* (Luke 15:10 NKJV).

They rejoice because Jesus heals those who are broken.

Likewise, God's people are to rejoice because the broken-hearted and emotionally wounded come to Him.

> *The Spirit of the Lord is upon Me, because He has anointed Me to preach the gospel to the poor; He has sent Me to heal the brokenhearted, to proclaim liberty to the captives and recovery of sight to the blind, to set at liberty those who are oppressed* (Luke 4:18 NKJV).

Christ unleashed power in the infirm woman that day. He healed her body and gave her the strength of character to keep a proper attitude. All who are broken and wounded today will find power unleashed within when they respond to the call and bring their wounds to the Great Physician.

Prayer

I offer You, the Great Physician, my humblest and most sincere gratitude for the healings You have blessed me with over the years. From a scratch that heals itself to the mental anguish that inevitably comes from life's bumps and bruises,

You have never neglected bringing me comfort and recovery. You are great and greatly to be praised. In Jesus's name, amen.

Declaration

**I believe in the Miracle Worker
who healed yesterday and heals
today and every tomorrow.**

Good and Perfect Gifts

Whatever is good and perfect is a gift coming down to us from God our Father, who created all the lights in the heavens. He never changes or casts a shifting shadow (James 1:17 NLT).

JESUS HEALED TEN LEPERS, and only one returned to Him (see Luke 17:11-19). When he came to Jesus, he fell down at His feet and worshipped Him. Then Jesus asked a question. It's seldom that Jesus, the omniscient One, would ask anything, but this time He had a question. I shall never forget the pointedness of His question. He asked the one who returned, "Where are the nine?"

Perhaps you are the one in ten who has the discernment to know that this blessing is nothing without the One who caused it all to happen. Most people are so concerned about their immediate needs that they fail to take the powerful experience that comes from a continued relationship with God! This is for the person who goes back to the Sender of gifts with the power of praise.

Ten men were healed, but to the one who returned, Jesus added the privilege of being whole. Many will climb the corporate ladder. Some will claim the accolades of this world. But soon all will realize that success, even with all its glamour, cannot heal a parched soul that needs the refreshment of a change of pace. Nothing can bring wholeness like the presence of a God who lingers on the road where He first blessed you to see if there is anything in you that would return you from the temporal to embrace the eternal.

Remember, healing can be found anywhere, but wholeness is achieved only when you go back to the Sender with all of your heart and thank Him for the miracle of a second chance. Whatever you do, don't forget your roots. When you can't go anywhere else, my friend, remember you can go home!

Prayer

Jesus, my Savior, I pray that I will be the one who will always return to thank You for all that You do for me—for my good health, family, friends, employment, the air I breathe and the water that nourishes me—but especially for the sacrifice You made on the Cross for my salvation. Thank You!

Declaration

I declare and believe that Jesus is the Son of God and that He reigns forevermore in Heaven.

Life

Whoever pursues righteousness and love finds life, prosperity and honor (Proverbs 21:21 NIV).

I HOPE YOU CAN RELATE to what a blessing it is to be alive, to be able to feel, to be able to taste life. Lift the glass to your mouth and drink deeply of life; it is a privilege to experience every drop of a human relationship. It is not perfect; like a suede jacket, the imperfection adds to its uniqueness. I am sure yours, like mine, is a mixing of good days, sad days, and all the challenges of life.

> *Pursue righteousness and a godly life, along with faith, love, perseverance, and gentleness* (1 Timothy 6:11 NLT).

I hope you have learned that a truly good relationship is a spicy meal served on a shaky table, filled with dreams and pains and tender moments. Moments that, in those split-second flashbacks, make you smile secret smiles in the middle of the day. Moments so strong that they never die, but yet are so fragile they disappear like bubbles in a glass. It does not matter whether you have something to be envied or something to be developed; if you can look back and catch a few moments, or trace a smile back to a memory, you are blessed! You could have been anywhere doing anything, but instead the *maitre d'* has seated you at a table for two!

Rather, he must enjoy having guests in his home, and he must love what is good. He must live wisely and be just. He must live a devout and disciplined life (Titus 1:8 NLT).

Come to me with your ears wide open. Listen, and you will find life. I will make an everlasting covenant with you. I will give you all the unfailing love I promised to David (Isaiah 55:3 NLT).

Prayer

Holy Giver of Life, from breathing Your breath into the first Adam until today when breathing life into each baby born, You are confirming how much You love each child You create. May I have the same compassion for those with whom I live and work and play. Grant me the joy of life that David had when he danced in the streets and that Mary had when she first looked into the face of the Christ Child. In that Child's name I pray, amen.

Declaration

I choose life!

Something Better

The woman then left her waterpot, went her way into the city, and said to the men, "Come, see a Man who told me all things that I ever did. Could this be the Christ?" Then they went out of the city and came to Him. ...And many of the Samaritans of that city believed in Him because of the word of the woman who testified, "He told me all that I ever did." So when the Samaritans had come to Him, they urged Him to stay with them; and He stayed there two days. And many more believed because of His own word. Then they said to the woman, "Now we believe, not because of what you said, for we ourselves have heard Him and we know that this is indeed the Christ, the Savior of the world" (John 4:28-30, 39-42 NKJV).

THIS WOMAN DIDN'T EVEN GO BACK HOME. She ran into the city telling everyone to come and see the Man who had told her about her life. You do yourself a disservice until you really come to know Jesus. He satisfies. Everyone else? Well, they pacify—but Jesus satisfies. He can satisfy every need and every yearning. He heals every pain and every affliction. Then He lifts every burden and every trouble in your life.

You have had enough tragedy. You have been bent over long enough. God will do something good in you. God kept you living through all those years of infirmity because He had something greater for you than what you experienced earlier. God kept you because He has something better for you.

You may have been abused and misused. Perhaps all those you trusted in turned on you and broke your heart. Still God has sustained you. You didn't make it because you were strong. You didn't make it because you were smart. You didn't make it because you were wise. *You made it because God's amazing grace kept you and sustained you.* God has more for you today than what you went through yesterday. Don't give up. Don't give in. Hold on. The blessing is on the way!

Prayer

Dear God, full of grace and mercy, thank You for the example of the Samaritan woman who was so excited to have met the Lord Jesus that she ran to tell everyone who would listen about the Man. She introduced Him to God knows how many that day, and for days to follow, the story of His presence spread. Lord, may I, too, share You and Your Son with others today and every day, with the help of the Holy Spirit. In Jesus's name, amen.

Declaration

I will run and shout out God's Good News!

God's Favor

"Why are you so angry?" the Lord asked Cain. "Why do you look so dejected? You will be accepted if you do what is right. But if you refuse to do what is right, then watch out! Sin is crouching at the door, eager to control you. But you must subdue it and be its master" (Genesis 4:6-7 NLT).

SOME PEOPLE ARE OFFENDED at what God does for you. I call those people "Cain's children." Cain's children, like their father, will murder you because you have God's favor. Watch out for them. They will not rejoice with you. They can't be glad for you because somehow they feel your success came at their expense. They foolishly believe that you have their blessing. No diplomacy can calm a jealous heart. They don't want to pay what you paid, but they want to have what you have.

It is amazing the relationships that can be lost as you travel upward. As long as you're in the day of small beginnings, you are acceptable. If you accelerate into new dimensions, however, cynicism eats at the fibers of their conversations and in their hearts. Your enemy will not wound you because he is too far way. In order to be a good Judas, he must be at the table with the victim of his betrayal!

Who sits at your table? Imagine Jesus, at the height of His ministerial career, sitting at the table with John, the beloved, on one side and Judas, the betrayer, on the other. The problem is in discerning which one is which. One of them is close enough to lay his head on your breast. The other has enough access to you to betray you with a kiss. They are both intimate, but one is lethal.

Keep your affections on the Giver and not the gifts. "Lord, help us to keep our eyes on what will not change." How many times have you prayed for a blessing? Then, when you received it, you realized there were strings attached that you didn't originally consider? To be honest, being blessed is hard work. Everything God gives you requires maintenance. God gave man the Garden, but the man still had to tend it. There is a "down" side to every blessing. That is why Jesus said, *"But don't begin until you count the cost. For who would begin construction of a building without first calculating the cost to see if there is enough money to finish it?"* (Luke 14:28 NLT). You must ask yourself if you are willing to pay the price to get the blessing.

Prayer

Father in Heaven, knowing that every blessing comes with a responsibility to tend to it, I will count the cost before asking—better yet, I will ask only if I believe it is Your will for me. In Jesus's name, I ask for discernment, Lord. Amen.

Declaration

I will seek God's favor, do what's right, and get rid of sin that may be at my door.

Steadfastness

*Jealousy arouses a husband's fury, and he will
show no mercy when he takes revenge. He will not
accept any compensation; he will refuse a bribe,
however great it is* (Proverbs 6:34-35 NIV).

DEAR FRIEND, as painful as it is to be criticized by those you
are in covenant with, it is far worse to give up the course that
God has for you just for their acceptance. In short, as much as
you need to be affirmed and understood, at some point you
must ask yourself, "How much am I willing to lose in order to
be accepted?" Truth be told, people do not always want to
see you move on—especially if they perceive you as moving
more rapidly than they are.

Can you endure the pressure they will put on you to come
down? Or will you be like Nehemiah, who said, *"I am doing
a great work, so that I cannot come down"* (Nehemiah 6:3
NKJV). Exaltation may cost you a degree of acceptance and
reward you with isolation. In fact, God may be grooming you
right now for a new level by exposing you to opposition and
criticism. He may be building up your immunity so when the
greater blessing comes, you won't break.

Successful people tend to be passionate people. These
are people who have intense desire. I admit there are many
passionate people who are not successful. But I didn't say
that passionate people are successful; I said that successful
people tend to be passionate. You can be passionate and

not be successful. Passion, basically, is raw power. If it is not harnessed and focused for a goal, it becomes an animalistic force. But if you can focus passion for a divine purpose, you will be successful. Some people never use their desire in a positive way.

Instead of harnessing passion and allowing it to become the force they use to overcome hindrances, it becomes a source of frustration and cynicism. Success only comes to a person who is committed to a cause or has a passion to achieve. Basically, the crux of the matter is: "How badly do you want to be blessed?"

Prayer

In the name of Jesus, Lord, I come to You with a request—to use me where and when You need me. May I be passionate for what You want to accomplish through me. May I be passionate enough to push away undeserved cynicism and criticism and focus on the life You chose for me to live.

Declaration

I will remain steadfast in my pursuit of God's blessing!

Vindication

*Instead, he [Jesus] gave up his divine privileges;
he took the humble position of a slave and was
born as a human being* (Philippians 2:7 NLT).

*Then the angel said to her, "Do not be afraid, Mary,
for you have found favor with God. And behold, you
will conceive in your womb and bring forth a Son,
and shall call His name Jesus"* (Luke 1:30-31 NKJV).

MARY, THE MOTHER OF JESUS, had the Baby, but the angel was sent from the Father to give the name. She couldn't name Him, because she didn't fully understand His destiny. Don't allow people who don't understand your destiny to name you. They also probably whispered that Jesus was the illegitimate Child of Joseph. Maybe there has been some nasty little rumor out on you too. Rumors smear the reputation and defame the character of many innocent people. However, none lived with any better moral character than Jesus—and they still assaulted His reputation. Just be sure the rumors are false or in the past, and keep on living. I often say, "You can't help where you've been, but you can help where you're going."

> *It came to pass in those days that Jesus came
> from Nazareth of Galilee, and was baptized by
> John in the Jordan. And immediately, coming
> up from the water, He saw the heavens parting*

and the Spirit descending upon Him like a dove. Then a voice came from heaven, "You are My beloved Son, in whom I am well pleased" (Mark 1:9-11 NKJV).

In the chilly river of Jordan, with mud between Jesus's toes, the voice of the Father declared the identity of Christ. His ministry could not begin until the Father laid hands upon Him by endorsing Him in the midst of the crowd. It is so important that we as God's children receive the blessing of our spiritual fathers. I know countless preachers who ran away from their spiritual homes without their fathers' blessings and, even after many years, are still in a turmoil. If Jesus needed His Father's blessing, how much more do you and I? We should not seek to endorse ourselves.

Prayer

Even Your sinless, innocent Son's reputation was smeared and His character defamed. No one lived with any better moral character than Jesus— and they still assaulted Him. Yet! You descended like a dove to vindicate Him after His baptism— and before a crowd who would tell of what they witnessed. You, God, are my Advocate too—thank You. In Jesus's name, amen.

Declaration

I can't help where I've been, but I will keep living for Christ alone.

God Provides

*Command those who are rich in this present world not to be arrogant nor to put their hope in wealth, which is so uncertain, but to put their hope in **God, who richly provides us with everything for our enjoyment*** (1 Timothy 6:17 NIV).

SATAN CANNOT DISPUTE our serving God, but he challenges our reason for serving Him. He says it is for the prominence and protection that God provides. He further insinuates that if things weren't going so well, we would not praise God so fervently. The devil is a liar!

In each of our lives, in one way or another, we will face times when we must answer satan's charges and prove that even in the storm, God is still God! Those early times of challenge sorely tried all that was in me. My pride, my self-esteem, and my self-confidence teetered like a child learning to ride a bicycle. My greatest fear was that it would never end. I feared that, like a person stuck in an elevator, I would spend the rest of my life between floors—neither here nor there in an intermediate stage of transition.

I felt like a shoulder out of joint and in pain. I learned, however, that if you can remember your beginnings and still reach toward your goals, God will bless you with things without fear of those items becoming idols in your life. Oddly, there is a glory in the agonizing of early years that people who didn't have to struggle seem not to possess. There is a strange sense of competence that comes from being born in the flames of struggle. How wildly exuberant are the first steps of the child who earlier was mobile only by crawling on his hands and knees.

If anyone speaks, they should do so as one who speaks the very words of God. If anyone serves, they should do so with **the strength God provides,** *so that in all things God may be praised through Jesus Christ. To him be the glory and the power for ever and ever. Amen* (1 Peter 4:11 NIV).

Prayer

My Provider God, my Jehovah Jireh, You provide all that I need, and I thank You for that. I'm sorry if I take for granted or don't appreciate all of Your abundant blessings. Forgive me. Your magnificent provision should never be dismissed—rather, each blessing should be accepted with the utmost gratitude and thankfulness. Forgive me, Lord. In Jesus's name, amen.

Declaration

**I thank God for His generosity
and His faithfulness!**

Maturity

Until we all reach unity in the faith and in the knowledge of the Son of God and become mature, attaining to the whole measure of the fullness of Christ (Ephesians 4:13 NIV).

MANY MISUNDERSTAND THE PROPHECIES of the Lord and so feel discontentment and despair. Just because God promises to move in your life and anoints you to do a particular function doesn't mean that your foundation will be immediately built. Directly after David was anointed to lead Israel, he was sent back into the field to feed the sheep. Joseph received a dream from the Lord that showed him ruling and reigning over his brothers, but in the next event, his brothers stripped him, beat him, and tossed him in a hole.

Can you imagine what the devil said to Joseph while he nursed his scrapes and bruises in the dark hole of small beginnings? Swallowed up with bruises and scars, he listened to the sound of depression sweeping through his throbbing head that beat like the congo drums of an African warrior. Satan's laugh filled the dark channels of the hole with his evil hysteria. "So you were going to reign, were you? I thought the dream said you were in charge," the enemy taunted. Satan didn't understand that all great prophecies start out small.

Picture chestnuts in the hand of a child. Those same chestnuts will one day be large enough to hold a child like the one who once held them. God has not changed His mind. His methods may seem crude, but His purpose is to provide wonderful success. Don't die in the hole! God hasn't changed His mind. He is a Master Builder, and He spends extra time laying a great foundation.

When the first Adam was created, he was created full grown. He had no childhood, no small things. He was just immediately a man. But when it was time for the last Adam (Jesus), God didn't create Him full grown. No, He took His time and laid a foundation. He was born a child and laid in a manger. The Manager of the universe was laid in a manger. *"For unto us a child is born, unto us a son is given"* (Isaiah 9:6 KJV). The Bible says that He grew in favor with God and man (see Luke 2:52). Not too fast, but He grew. Please allow yourself time to mature.

Prayer

You are the Master Builder, and I trust You to be working on building my life into the one You designed. Learning from people in the Bible, I realize that time is involved in maturing into Your will and living according to Your perfect plan. Give me patience, Lord, to remain resolute on my journey of faith. In Jesus's name, amen.

Declaration

I believe that as I mature, God's purpose is to provide wonderful success for me.

Friendships

*When we get together, I want to encourage
you in your faith, but I also want to be
encouraged by yours* (Romans 1:12 NLT).

*Then Elimelech died, and Naomi was left with her
two sons. ... about ten years later, both Mahlon
and Kilion died. This left Naomi alone, without
her two sons or her husband* (Ruth 1:3-5 NLT).

RUTH WAS NAOMI'S DAUGHTER-IN-LAW. Naomi thought
their only connection was her now dead son. Many times
we, who have been very family-oriented, do not understand
friendships. When family circumstances change, we lapse
into isolation because we know nothing of other relationships. *"A man who has friends must himself be friendly, but
there is a friend who sticks closer than a brother"* (Proverbs
18:24 NKJV).

There are bonds that are stronger than blood. They are
God-bonds! When God brings someone into our life, He is the
Bonding Agent. Ruth said, "Your God shall be my God." God
wanted Naomi to see the splendor of winter relationships,
the joy of passing the baton of her wisdom and strength to
someone worthy of her attention.

Let God choose such a person for us because too often
we choose on the basis of fleshly ties and not godly ties. I

have noticed in the Scriptures that the strongest female relationships tend to be exemplified between older and younger women. I am certainly not suggesting that such will always be the case. Ruth would have died in Moab, probably marrying some heathenistic idolator, if it were not for the wisdom of Naomi, an older, more seasoned woman.

Naomi knew how to provide guidance without manipulation—a strength many women at that stage of life do not have. Ruth was, of course, one of the great-grandparents in the lineage of Jesus Christ. She had greatness in her that God used Naomi to cultivate. Perhaps Naomi would have been called Mara, and perhaps she would have ended up dying in bitterness instead of touching lives—if it had not been for Ruth.

Prayer

Dear God, I welcome more friends. I look forward to those You will place in my path who can encourage me and I them. Friends are Your gift—over the past years, some have been long-term, and others have floated in and out of my life. I depend on You to bring people who will stick close—to me and You! In the precious name of Your Son, my Friend, amen.

Declaration

I will be friendly to attract the friends God puts in my life.

Guidance

Similarly, encourage the young men to be self-controlled. In everything set them an example by doing what is good. In your teaching show integrity, seriousness (Titus 2:6-7 NIV).

GOD WILL GIVE YOU whatever you ask for (see John 14:13). God will give you a business. God will give you a dream. He will make you the head and not the tail (see Deuteronomy 28:13). God's power brings all things up under your feet. Believe Him for your household. God will deliver. You don't need a sugar daddy. You have Jehovah Jireh, the best Provider this world has ever known.

"So in Christ Jesus you are all children of God through faith" (Galatians 3:26 NIV). Women are just as much children of God as men are. Everything God will do for a man, He will do for a woman. You are not disadvantaged. You can get an inheritance like any man. Generally, men don't cry about being single—they simply get on with life and stay busy. There is no reason a woman can't be complete in God without a husband.

If you choose to get married, you should get married for the right reasons. Don't give in to a desperate spirit that forces you to put up with someone less than who you want. You could become stuck with an immature man and then birth three little boys. Then you would have four little boys. That is no way to live.

You need someone who has some shoulders and a back-bone. You need to marry someone who will hold you, help you, strengthen you, build you up, and be with you when the storms of life are raging. If you want a cute man, buy a photograph. If you want some help, marry a godly man.

> *But you, Timothy, are a man of God; so run from all these evil things. Pursue righteousness and a godly life, along with faith, love, perseverance, and gentleness* (1 Timothy 6:11 NLT).

Prayer

Almighty, I look to You for guidance in all areas of my life, knowing that You know my end from my beginning. Lead me onto Your perfect path that takes me toward an abundant life filled with blessings galore. In Jesus's name, amen.

Declaration

I claim the favor of God for me and my family!

His Embrace

One day some parents brought their children to Jesus so he could touch and bless them. But the disciples scolded the parents for bothering him. When Jesus saw what was happening, he was angry with his disciples. He said to them, "Let the children come to me. Don't stop them! For the Kingdom of God belongs to those who are like these children. I tell you the truth, anyone who doesn't receive the Kingdom of God like a child will never enter it." Then he took the children in his arms and placed his hands on their heads and blessed them (Mark 10:13-16 NLT).

WHAT WAS WRONG with these disciples that they became angry at parents who aimed their children toward the only Answer they might have ever seen? He told the little children to come to Him, and He stopped His message for His mission.

Imagine tiny hands outstretched, little faces upturned, small forms perching like sparrows on His knee. They came to get a touch, but He always gives us more than we expect. He held them with His loving arms. He touched with His sensitive hands. But most of all, He blessed them with His compassionate heart! I am concerned that we maintain our compassion. How can we be in the presence of a loving God and not love little ones?

When Jesus blessed the children, He challenged the adults to become as children. Oh, to be a child again, to allow ourselves the kind of relationship with God that we might have missed as a child. Sometimes we need to allow the Lord to adjust the damaged places of our past. I am glad to say that the arms of God allow grown children to climb up like young children and be nurtured through the tragedies of early days. Isn't it nice to toddle into the presence of God and let Him hold you in His arms?

In God, we can become children again. Salvation is God giving us a chance to start over again. He will not abuse the children who come to Him. Through praise, I approach Him like a toddler on unskillful legs. In worship, I kiss His face and am held by the caress of His anointing. He has no ulterior motive, for His caress is safe and wholesome. It is so important that we learn how to worship and adore Him. There is no better way to climb into His arms.

Prayer

Abba Father, to praise You like a child and worship You with a kiss is my desire. I adore You, Lord, for the loving and compassionate God You are. May I never shoo away children or immature believers when they need me to be an example of Your safe and wholesome presence. This I pray in Jesus's name, amen.

Declaration

I will praise and worship my heavenly Father as a child full of excitement!

Wealth

You say, "I am rich; I have acquired wealth and do not need a thing." But you do not realize that you are wretched, pitiful, poor, blind and naked (Revelation 3:17 NIV).

WHAT WE ALL NEED is the unique gift of acceptance. Most of us fear the bitter taste of rejection, but perhaps worse than rejection is the naked pain that attacks an exposed heart when a relationship is challenged by some struggle.

Suppose I share my heart, my innermost thoughts, with someone who betrays me, and I am wounded again? The distress of betrayal can become a wall that insulates us, but it also isolates us from those around us. Yes, I must admit that there are good reasons for being protective and careful. I also admit that love is always a risk. Yet I still suggest that the risk is worth the reward! What a privilege to have savored the contemplations of idle moments with the tender eyes of someone whose glistening expression invites you like the glowing embers of a crackling fire.

Communication becomes needless between people who need no audible speech. Their speech is the quick glance and the soft pat on a shoulder. Their communication is a concerned glance when all is not well with you. If you have ever sunk down into the rich lather of a real covenant relationship, then you are wealthy.

This relationship is the wealth that causes street people to smile in the rain and laugh in the snow. They have no coats to warm them; their only flame is the friendship of someone who relates to the plight of daily living. In this regard, many wealthy people are impoverished. They have things, but they lack camaraderie. The greatest blessings are often void of expense, yet they provide memories that enrich the credibility of life's dreary existence.

Prayer

Yes, Lord! In Jesus's name I pray that You will show me my real worth and the riches You provide that outshine all the worldly glitter that catches my eye and wastes my time. I look to You for the greatest blessings that are free for the asking—in and from You.

Declaration

My wealth comes from my intimate relationship with the Lord Jesus Christ.

A Judas

The Lord is with me; I will not be afraid. What can mere mortals do to me? (Psalm 118:6 NIV).

GOD HAS USED CERTAIN "FRIENDS" and their negativity to accomplish His will for our lives. Because our ultimate goal is to please Him, we must widen our definition of friendship to include the betrayer if his betrayal ushers us into the next step of God's plan for our lives.

> *So Judas came straight to Jesus. "Greetings, Rabbi!" he exclaimed and gave him the kiss. Jesus said, "My friend, go ahead and do what you have come for." Then the others grabbed Jesus and arrested him. But one of the men with Jesus pulled out his sword and struck the high priest's slave, slashing off his ear. "Put away your sword," Jesus told him. "Those who use the sword will die by the sword. Don't you realize that I could ask my Father for thousands of angels to protect us, and he would send them instantly? But if I did, how would the Scriptures be fulfilled that describe what must happen now?"* (Matthew 26:49-54 NLT).

I understand that in its narrow sense, a "friend" has good intentions. However, because of the sovereignty of God, I have come to realize that there are some who were actually instrumental in my blessing, although they never really embraced or affirmed me as a person! They played a crucial part in my well-being. These kinds of "friends" are the "Judas sector" that exists in the life of every child of God.

Every child of God not only has but also desperately needs a "Judas" to carry out certain aspects of divine providence in their life! In the passage quoted above, Judas was more of a friend than Peter! Although Peter was certainly more amiable and admirable, Judas was the one God selected to usher in the next step of the process. Peter's love was almost a deterrent to the purpose of God. Sometimes your friends can cause you the most pain. They wound you and betray you, but through their betrayal God's will can be executed in your life.

Prayer

When reading Your Word about Jesus and the role Judas played in His life, I realize that You can use anyone at anytime to fulfill Your purpose. Thinking back over my life, there have been people who aggravated and/or caused me pain. Maybe that was intentional and necessary to move me forward. I trust You. In Jesus's name, amen.

Declaration

I trust God to bring people into and out of my life as He deems necessary.

Individuality

*You watched me as I was being formed in
utter seclusion, as I was woven together in
the dark of the womb* (Psalm 139:15 NLT).

PUT THE TRUTH IN YOUR SPIRIT, and feed, nurture, and allow it to grow. Quit telling yourself, "You're too fat, too old, too late, or too ignorant." Quit feeding yourself that garbage. That will not nourish the baby. Too often we starve the embryo of faith that is growing within us. It is unwise to speak against your own body.

Women tend to speak against their bodies, opening the door for sickness and disease. Speak life to your own body. Celebrate who you are. You are the image of God. Scriptures remind us of who we are: *"Thank you for making me so wonderfully complex! Your workmanship is marvelous—how well I know it"* (Psalm 139:14 NLT). These are the words that will feed our souls.

The truth allows new life to swell up within us. Feed the faith embryo within with such words as these:

> *When I look at the night sky and see the work of your fingers—the moon and the stars you set in place—what are mere mortals that you should think about them, human beings that you should care for them?* (Psalm 8:3-4 NLT).

The Lord will make you the head and not the tail, and you will always be on top and never at the bottom (Deuteronomy 28:13 NLT).

I can do everything through Christ, who gives me strength (Philippians 4:13 NLT).

The Word of God provides the nourishment that feeds the baby of faith inside.

Prayer

Although I know I am fearfully and wonderfully made by You, Creator God, I tend to think of that as the spiritual me. The physical me finds flaws—new ones almost daily. Lord, in Jesus's name, I turn those complaints and disappointments regarding my appearance over to You. Help me see me as You see me—made in Your perfect image.

Declaration

I am made in the image of my Lord and Savior, and I will be content spiritually and physically.

Faith to See

Faith is confidence in what we hope for and assurance about what we do not see. This is what the ancients were commended for. By faith we understand that the universe was formed at God's command, so that what is seen was not made out of what was visible (Hebrews 11:1-3 NIV).

THE BOOK OF HEBREWS provides us with a tremendous lesson on faith. When we believe God, we are counted as righteous. Righteousness cannot be earned or merited. It comes only through faith. We can have a good report simply on the basis of our faith. Faith becomes the tender, like money is the legal tender in this world that we use for exchange of goods and services. Faith becomes the tender, or the substance, of things hoped for and the evidence of things not seen.

> *By it* [faith] *the elders obtained a good testimony* (Hebrews 11:2 NKJV).

> *By faith we understand that the worlds were framed by the word of God, so that things which are seen were not made of things which are visible* (Hebrews 11:3 NKJV).

The invisible became visible and was manifested. God wants us to understand that just because we can't see it doesn't mean that He won't do it. What God wants to do in us begins as a word that gets in the spirit. Everything that is tangible started as an intangible. It was a dream, a thought, a word of God. In the same way, what humans have invented began as a concept in someone's mind. Faith.

> **By faith** Abel offered to God a more excellent sacrifice than Cain, through which he obtained witness that he was righteous, God testifying of his gifts; and through it he being dead still speaks. **By faith** Enoch was taken away so that he did not see death, "and was not found, because God had taken him"; for before he was taken he had this testimony, that he pleased God (Hebrews 11:4-5 NKJV).

Prayer

By faith, I come before You now, God, to surrender myself to Your will and way—to what I see and don't see. Open my spiritual eyes to see what You want to show me, and may I use those sights to help Your Kingdom to come on earth as it is in Heaven. Grant me the faith to see You in everything and everyone around me. Thank You in Jesus's name. Amen.

Declaration

By faith I believe!

Your Everything

For the Lord your God has blessed you in everything you have done. He has watched your every step through this great wilderness. During these forty years, the Lord your God has been with you, and you have lacked nothing (Deuteronomy 2:7 NLT).

IF YOU ARE LOOKING for someone to be your everything, don't look around—look up! God is the only One who can be everything.

By expecting perfection from the flesh, you ask more out of someone else than what you can provide yourself. To be married is to have a partner: someone who is not always there or always on target or always anything! On the other hand, should you ever get in trouble and you don't know who to look to for help, you can count on your spouse—someone to curl up against when the world seems cold and life uncertain. Someone who is as concerned as you are when your children are ill. A hand that keeps checking your forehead when you aren't well.

To be married is to have someone's shoulder to cry on as they lower your parent's body into the ground. It is to wrap wrinkled knees in warm blankets and to giggle without teeth! To the person you marry, you are saying, "When my time comes to leave this world, and the chill of eternity blows away my birthdays, and my future stands still in the night, it's your face I want to kiss goodbye. It is your hand I want to squeeze as I slip from time into eternity. As the curtain closes on all I have attempted to do and be, I want to look into your eyes and see that I mattered. Not what I looked like. Not what I did or how much money I made. Not even how talented I was. I want to look into the teary eyes of someone who loved me and see that I mattered!"

If you are married or not, though, God is the only One who will be there every moment of every day—right next to you, loving you more than anyone on earth could possibly love you. You have mattered to Him from the moment He chose to form you in His mind, then in your mother's womb. He has always been your everything.

Prayer

Dear Almighty Everything, thank You for being all that I ever need, want, expect, and yearn for in life. I will stop looking around, and keep looking up— up to Heaven where You wait for me to join You some glorious day! In Jesus's name, let it be so.

Declaration

Jesus is everything I've ever dreamed of and more!

Rest

Many people say, "Who will show us better times?" Let your face smile on us, Lord. You have given me greater joy than those who have abundant harvests of grain and new wine. In peace I will lie down and sleep, for you alone, O Lord, will keep me safe (Psalm 4:6-8 NLT).

I DARE YOU to realize that you can do all things through Christ who strengthens you (see Philippians 4:13). Once the infirm woman knew that she didn't have to be bent over, she stood straight up. Jesus told the woman at the well to get rid of the old. He wanted her to step away from that old pattern of selfishness. Suddenly, she recognized that she didn't have what she thought she had. The sinful things that you have fought to maintain are not worth what you thought they were.

I'm referring to some of those things that have attached themselves to your life in which you find comfort. Some of those habits you came to enjoy, some of those relationships you thought you found security in, were not profitable. Often we settle for less because we didn't meet the best. When you get the best, it gives you the power to let go of the rest.

The infirm woman Jesus healed in Luke 13 didn't panic because of her crippling disease. She had been in torment and pain for 18 years. When she came into the presence of Jesus, she relaxed in Him. She expected that He would take care of her. The result was a wonderful healing. The woman at the well from John 4 expected water, but she left the well having found the Savior. She sought temporal satisfaction—but found eternal satisfaction.

That's what rest and Sabbath is. It is the ability to find eternal satisfaction in Jesus. The world will never give us peace and satisfaction. Jesus offers both freely.

If you have struggled to find satisfaction, you can find hope for your soul in the Master of the universe. He will not deny you because of your past. He will not scrutinize your every action. He will take you as you are and give you rest. He will provide a peace that will satisfy the every yearning of your soul.

Prayer

I agree with the psalmist, Lord: "You have given me greater joy than those who have abundant harvests of grain and new wine. In peace I will lie down and sleep, for you alone, O Lord, will keep me safe." I pray that Your countenance will shine upon me. In Jesus's name, amen.

Declaration

Only God can give me total peace, satisfaction, and rest.

Struggles

The master said, "Well done, my good and faithful servant. You have been faithful in handling this small amount, so now I will give you many more responsibilities. Let's celebrate together!" (Matthew 25:23 NLT).

YOU MUST ASK YOURSELF if you are willing to pay the price to get the blessing. Another question people seldom ask themselves is whether they are willing to endure the criticism, ridicule, and struggles that come with success.

With this we have already weeded out half the people who say they want something from the Lord. We have weeded out all the women who say they want a husband and children but don't want to cook, care, or clean. We have weeded out all the men who say they want a wife but don't want to love, provide, and nourish!

Most people are in love with the image of success, but they haven't contemplated the reality of possessing the blessing. It is a good thing God doesn't give us everything we ask for, because we want some things simply because they look good in someone else's life. The truth is, we are not ready for those things, and it would probably kill us to receive what we are not prepared to maintain.

So you're whimsically toying with the idea of exercising your ability to receive a blessing? This is a good place to start. I believe that God starts His children out with what they have, so He can teach consistency on the level they are on. There must be an inner growth in your ability to withstand the struggles that accompany the things you have. I am so glad that God allowed me to go through the pain-ridden days of stress and rejection early in my life.

I found out that if you really want to pursue your dream, there is a place in God whereby you build up an immunity to the adversity of success. It is simply a matter of survival. Either you become immune to the criticism and confusing pressures and isolation, or you go absolutely stark raving, mouth-foaming mad!

Prayer

Oh heavenly Father, how I look forward to hearing You say, "Well done, My good and faithful servant"—be it here on earth or in Heaven when I see You face to face. I am ready for more responsibilities now, if You think so as well—and I'm ready to celebrate together with You!

Declaration

I am a good and faithful servant for my Lord and Savior, Almighty God.

Survival Skills

For in the day of trouble he [God] *will keep me safe in his dwelling; he will hide me in the shelter of his sacred tent and set me high upon a rock* (Psalm 27:5 NIV).

IF YOU ARE ALWAYS weeping over rejection and misunderstanding, if you're always upset over who doesn't accept you into their circles anymore, you may be suffering from an immunity deficiency syndrome. You waste precious time of communion when you ask God to change the minds of people. It is not the people or the pressure that must change—it is you. In order to survive the stresses of success, you must build up an immunity to those things that won't change.

Thank God that He provides elasticity for us. Remember, you can't switch price tags just because you don't like the price. My constant prayer is, "Lord, change me until this doesn't hurt anymore." I am like David—I am forever praying my way into the secret place. The secret place in the king's court was called a pavilion: *"For in the time of trouble He shall hide me in His pavilion; in the secret place of His tabernacle He shall hide me; He shall set me high upon a rock"* (Psalm 27:5 NKJV). There you are insulated from the enemy. If you can make it to the secret place, all hell could break loose outside, but it will not matter to you, for in His sanctuary is peace. If you want to accomplish much, if you intend to survive Cain's hateful children, you need to get in the secret place and stay there!

What a place of solace God has for the weary heart bombarded with the criticism of cynical people and the pressures to perform. I often think of how many times I allowed to overwhelm me things that really didn't make any difference. In retrospect, half of the things I was praying about should have been dismissed as trivialities. Maturity is sweet relief for those who haven't yet learned how to survive the blessings God has given them. I know that sounds strange, but many people don't survive their own success.

Notoriety comes and goes, but when it is over, you want to still be around. Many people lose their own identities in the excitement of the moment. When the excitement ebbs, as it always does, they have lost sight of the more important issues of God, self, home, and family!

Prayer

Thank You, God, for saving me from myself—for not allowing me to be swept away with success that could easily have led me astray. Thank You for providing a secret place where I can survive the trouble, while at the same time returning my focus to You, family, and others. I praise Your holy, sacred name. Amen.

Declaration

I declare today that I will not try and change people's minds about me—but rather change my mind to what God says is important.

Mercy

But you are not like that, for you are a chosen people. You are royal priests, a holy nation, God's very own possession. As a result, you can show others the goodness of God, for he called you out of the darkness into his wonderful light. "Once you had no identity as a people; now you are God's people. Once you received no mercy; now you have received God's mercy" (1 Peter 2:9-10 NLT).

RAHAB WAS A HARLOT until she found faith. *"By faith the harlot Rahab perished not with them that believed not, when she had received the spies with peace"* (Hebrews 11:31 KJV). Once she had faith, she no longer turned to her old profession.

The infirmed woman in Luke 13 was stooped over until Jesus touched her. Once He touched her, she stood up. When you put on Christ, there is no reason to be bent over after His touch. You can walk with respect even when you have past failures. It's not what people say about you that makes you different. It is what you say about yourself, and what your God has said about you, that really matters.

Just because someone calls you a tramp doesn't mean you have to act like one. Rahab walked with respect. You will find her name mentioned in the lineage of Jesus Christ. She went from being a prostitute to being one of the great-grand-mothers of our Lord and Savior, Jesus Christ. *You can't help where you've been, but you can help where you're going.*

God is not concerned about race. He is not concerned if you're Black. You may think, *My people came over on a boat and picked cotton on a plantation.* It doesn't make any difference. The answer isn't to be White. Real spiritual advantage does not come from the color of your skin. It's not the color of your skin that will bring deliverance and help from God—it's the contents of your heart.

Prayer

Lord, I believe that You have made me part of Your chosen people, a holy nation, Your very own possession. Help me to show others Your goodness so as to pull them out of the darkness into Your wonderful light and mercy. I ask this in the lovely name of Jesus, amen.

Declaration

**What God says about me is
what matters most.**

Advantages

I want you to be free from the concerns of this life. An unmarried man can spend his time doing the Lord's work and thinking how to please him. But a married man has to think about his earthly responsibilities and how to please his wife. His interests are divided. In the same way, a woman who is no longer married or has never been married can be devoted to the Lord and holy in body and in spirit. But a married woman has to think about her earthly responsibilities and how to please her husband (1 Corinthians 7:32-34 NLT).

SOME BELIEVERS DO NOT understand the benefits of being single. In reality, while you're not married, you really ought to be involved with God. When you get married, you direct all of the training that you had while you were unmarried toward your spouse.

The apostle Paul addressed this issue in his first letter to the church at Corinth. Single women often forget some very important advantages they have. At five o'clock in the morning, you can lie in bed and pray in the Spirit till seven-thirty and not have to answer to anyone. You can worship the Lord whenever and however you please. You can lie prostrate on the floor in your house and worship, and no one will become annoyed about it.

"A woman who is no longer married or has never been married can be devoted to the Lord and holy in body and in

spirit." Often those who minister in churches hear unmarried women complain about their need for a husband, but rarely does a single woman boast about the kind of relationship she is free to build with the Lord.

Are you complaining about how you need someone? Take advantage of the time you don't have to worry about cooking meals and caring for a family. While a woman is single, she needs to recognize that she has the unique opportunity to build herself up in the Lord without the drains that can occur later.

Prayer

Heavenly Father, may I use my time wisely—devoting space in my life for studying Your Word, listening for Your Word, meditating on Your Word, and going about my daily work for You as my first priority. When I put You at the top of my mind and spirit, all else will fall perfectly into place. In Jesus's name, let it be so.

Declaration

**I am devoted to the Lord—
body, mind, and spirit.**

Grace

Each time he said, "My grace is all you need.
My power works best in weakness." So now
I am glad to boast about my weaknesses,
so that the power of Christ can work
through me (2 Corinthians 12:9 NLT).

JESUS CONCLUDED THAT the rejections He experienced were the doings of the Lord! As Joseph so aptly put it, *"You intended to harm me, but God intended it all for good"* (Genesis 50:20 NLT). The Lord orchestrates what the enemy does and makes it accomplish His purpose in your life. This is the Lord's doing! How many times have "evil" things happened in your life that later you realized were necessary? If I hadn't faced trials like these, I know that I wouldn't have been ready for the blessings I now enjoy.

In the hands of God, even our most painful circumstances become marvelous in our eyes! When we see how perfectly God has constructed His plan, we can laugh in the face of failure. However, *rejection is only marvelous in the eyes of someone whose heart has wholly trusted in the Lord!*

Have you wholly trusted in the Lord, or are you grieving over something that someone has done—as though you have no God to direct it and no grace to correct it? This is an important question because it challenges the perspectives you have chosen to take for your life.

Jesus said to them, "Have you never read in the Scriptures: 'The stone which the builders rejected has become the chief cornerstone. This was the Lord's doing, and it is marvelous in our eyes'?" (Matthew 21:42 NKJV).

"It is marvelous in our eyes" simply means that from our perspective, the worst things look good! That is what you need faith to do! Faith is not needed just to remove problems; it is also needed to *endure* problems that seem immovable. Rest assured that even if God didn't move it, He is able! If your able God chose to stand passively by and watch someone come whose actions left you in pain, you still must trust in His sovereign grace and immutable character. He works for your good. Someone wrote a song that said, "If life hands you a lemon, just make lemonade." That's cute, but the truth is—if you walk with God, He will do the squeezing and the mixing that turn lemons into lemonade!

Prayer

In Jesus's name, Lord, I will wholly trust You. I wholly believe that You're the God of grace and mercy— more than able to bring good from the not-so-good in my life. I trust in Your sovereign grace and immutable character, knowing that You love me.

Declaration

**Jesus loves me! This I know,
for the Bible tells me so!**

Assurance

For in Scripture it says: "See, I lay a stone in Zion, a chosen and precious cornerstone, and the one who trusts in him will never be put to shame." Now to you who believe, this stone is precious. But to those who do not believe, "The stone the builders rejected has become the cornerstone" (1 Peter 2:6-7 NIV).

NORMALLY, ANYTIME THERE IS A CRASH, there is an injury. If one person collides with another, they generally damage everything associated with them. In the same way, a crashing relationship affects everyone associated with it, whether it is in a corporate office, a ministry, or a family. That jarring and shaking can damage everyone involved. Whether we like to admit it or not, we are affected by the actions of others to various degrees. The amount of the effect, though, depends on the nature of the relationship.

What is important is the fact that we don't have to die in the crashes and collisions of life. We must learn to live life with a seat belt in place, even though it is annoying to wear. Similarly, we need spiritual and emotional seat belts as well. We don't need the kind that harness us in and make us live like a mannequin; rather, we need the kind that are invisible—but greatly appreciated in a crash.

Inner assurance is the seat belt that stops you from going through the roof when you are rejected. It is inner *assurance* that holds you in place. It is the *assurance* that God is in control and that what He has determined no one can disallow! If He said He was going to bless you, then disregard the mess and believe the God who cannot lie. The rubbish can be cleared, and the bruises can be healed. Just be sure that when the smoke clears, you are still standing. You are too important to the purpose of God to be destroyed by a situation that is meant only to give you character and direction. No matter how painful, devastated, or disappointed you may feel, you are still here. Praise God, for *He will use the cornerstone developed through rejections and failed relationships to perfect what He has prepared!*

Lift your voice above the screaming sirens and alarms of men whose hearts have panicked! Lift your eyes above the billowing smoke and spiraling emotions. Pull yourself up—it could have killed you, but it didn't. Announce to yourself, "I am alive. I can laugh. I can cry, and by God's grace, I can survive!"

Prayer

Accept this song by Fanny Crosby as my prayer to You, Lord: "Blessed assurance, Jesus is mine! Oh, what a foretaste of glory divine! Heir of salvation, purchase of God, born of His Spirit, washed in His blood. This is my story, this is my song, praising my Savior all the day long; this is my story, this is my song." Amen and amen!

Declaration

**I am alive. I can laugh. I can cry, and
by God's grace, I can survive!**

Affirmation

I baptize you with water for repentance. But after me comes one who is more powerful than I, whose sandals I am not worthy to carry. He will baptize you with the Holy Spirit and fire. His winnowing fork is in his hand, and he will clear his threshing floor, gathering his wheat into the barn and burning up the chaff with unquenchable fire (Matthew 3:11-12 NIV).

LET ME WARN YOU: God places His prize possessions in the fire. The precious vessels that He draws the most brilliant glory from often are exposed to the melting pot of distress. The bad news is, even those who live godly lives will suffer persecution. The good news is, you might be in the fire, but God controls the thermostat! He knows how hot it needs to be to accomplish His purpose in your life. I don't know anyone I would rather trust with the thermostat than the God of all grace.

Every test has degrees. Some people have experienced similar distresses—but to varying degrees. God knows the temperature that will burn away the impurities from His purpose. It is sad to have to admit this, but many times we release the ungodliness from our lives only as we experience the dread chastisement of a faithful God who is committed to bringing about change. How often He has had to fan the flames around me to produce the effects that He wanted in my life. In short, God is serious about producing the change in our lives that will glorify Him.

For his Spirit joins with our spirit to affirm that we are God's children (Romans 8:16 NLT).

His hand has fanned the flames that were needed to teach patience, prayer, and many other invaluable lessons. We need His corrections. We don't enjoy them, but we need them. Without the correction of the Lord, we continue in our own way. What a joy to know that He cares enough to straighten out the jagged places in our lives. It is His fatherly corrections that confirm us as legitimate sons and not illegitimate ones. *He affirms my position in Him by correcting and chastening me.*

Prayer

Dear God, as Your prized possession, a precious vessel, let me not be surprised that I am exposed to the melting pot of distress. Thank You for controlling the thermostat, knowing how hot it needs to be to accomplish Your purpose in my life. Burn away the impurities, and fan the flames around me to produce the effects You want in me. In Jesus's name, amen.

Declaration

**Through God's flames of instruction,
He will teach me valuable lessons.**

Trust

*Those who live in the shelter of the Most High will find rest in the shadow of the Almighty. This I declare about the Lord: He alone is my refuge, my place of safety; he is my God, and **I trust him** (Psalm 91:1-2 NLT).*

THE BASIS OF ANY RELATIONSHIP must be trust. Trusting God with your successes isn't really a challenge. The real test of trust is to be able to share your secrets, your inner failures and fears. A mutual enhancement comes into a relationship where there is intimacy based on honesty.

Jesus told the woman at the well, a woman whose flaws and failures He had supernaturally revealed, "True worshipers will worship the Father in the Spirit and in truth, for they are the kind of worshipers the Father seeks. God is spirit, and his worshipers must worship in the Spirit and in truth" (John 4:23-24 NIV).

We have nothing to fear, for our honesty with the Father doesn't reveal anything to Him that He doesn't already know! His intellect is so keen that He doesn't have to wait for you to make a mistake. He knows of your failure before you fail. His knowledge is all-inclusive, spanning the gaps between times and incidents. He knows our thoughts even as we unconsciously gather them together to make sense in our own mind!

The Lord knows all human plans; he knows that they are futile (Psalm 94:11 NIV).

The Lord knoweth the thoughts of man, that they are vanity (Psalm 94:11 KJV).

Once we know this, all our attempts at silence and secrecy seem juvenile and ridiculous. He is "the all-seeing One," and He knows perfectly and completely what is in us. When we pray—and more importantly, when we commune with God—we must have the kind of confidence and assurance that neither requires nor allows deceit. Although my Father abhors my sin, He loves me. His love is incomprehensible, primarily because there is nothing with which we can compare! What we must do is accept the riches of His grace and stand in the shade of His loving arms.

Prayer

I trust You, God, with not only my successes but also my secrets, inner failures, and fears—my deepest hurts, angers, and worries. I pray, Lord, that I will open my heart and mind to create the type of intimacy based on honesty that You desire in our relationship. I know that You hate the sin that creeps in between us—stand guard, please; watch over me. I pray as David prayed, *"O Lord my God, in You I put my trust; save me from all those who persecute me; and deliver me."* (Psalm 7:1 NKJV) In Jesus's name, amen.

Declaration

I trust God's mercy. My heart
rejoices in His salvation.

Accountability

Nothing in all creation is hidden from God. Everything is naked and exposed before his eyes, and he is the one to whom we are accountable (Hebrews 4:13 NLT).

WE ARE CALLED TO live in a state of openhearted communication with the Lord. Yes, we feel vulnerable when we realize that our heart is completely exposed before God. Yet every one of us desperately needs to have *someone* who is able to help us, *someone* who is able to understand the issues that are etched on the tablets of our heart!

Since we already feel exposed when we realize there is not one thought we have entertained that God has not seen and heard, then *there is no need for a sanctimonious misrepresentation of who we are!* We no longer need to live under the strain of continual camouflage. Neither flagrant nor flamboyant, we are *naked before Him* in the same sense that a man sprawls naked on the operating table before a surgeon. The man is neither boastful nor embarrassed, for he understands that his exposed condition is a necessity of their relationship. Whether the doctor finds good or evil, the man's comfort lies in the conviction that the surgeon possesses the wherewithal to restore order to any area that may be in disarray.

"Blessed are the pure in heart, for they shall see God" (Matthew 5:8 NKJV). The purity that attracts the presence of God comes from allowing Him to perpetually flush away the corrosion that threatens to block the abundant arterial flow

of His grace and mercy toward us. In short, we need to show Him what is clogging or hindering His flow of life to us, so He can clean us and keep us acceptable before Him in love.

The Greek word *katheros* is used here to express "purity." It is from this word that we have the English derivative *catharize*, which describes medical processes used to cleanse, flush, or release fluids from the body. God is continually sending a deluge of His cleansing grace into the hearts of His children, *but He can't clean or purify what we hide in the secret corners of our hearts and minds.*

Prayer

Oh Lord, Your omnipotence is comforting yet terrifying at the same time. I realize nothing in all creation is hidden from God. Everything is naked and exposed before Your eyes. I realize that I am accountable to You, and I feel so unworthy. But! I also realize that Your mercy and grace extend to the depths of my being—and Your blood washes me as white as pure snow. Thank You—in Jesus's name! Amen.

Declaration

I will stop hiding what needs to be exposed, so God can clean and purify me.

Cleansing

"Come now, and let us reason together," says the Lord, "Though your sins are like scarlet, they shall be as white as snow; though they are red like crimson, they shall be as wool" (Isaiah 1:18 NKJV).

THE HYMNIST JAMES NICHOLSON wrote a powerful verse when he penned these lyrics in the song "Whiter Than Snow": "Lord Jesus, I long to be perfectly whole; I want Thee forever to live in my soul; break down every idol, cast out every foe—now wash me, and I shall be whiter than snow."

I can still remember the great joy that flooded my soul when Christ came into my heart. I was walking on air for weeks. It was and, in fact, still is exciting to me to know that my many deplorable sins have been rinsed from my records by the efficacious blood of the Lamb! I shouted and praised the Lord with abandonment, as if it were the last opportunity I would have to praise the Lord.

Upon reflection, I came to understand that the slate had been cleansed at Calvary, but the *mind* is being renewed from day to day. As images came from time to time with flashbacks of things that haunted the attic of my mind like ghosts unexorcised, I began to seek the Lord *who saved me* for *the grace to keep me*. It was then that I began to realize the great truth that the blood of Christ doesn't just reach backward into the bleakness of my past debauchery—it also has the power to cover my ongoing struggles!

I hadn't known then that Jesus paid it all! The blood of Christ covers my past, present, and future struggles, not so I can run through my inheritance like the prodigal son (if that were possible) but so I might have a comfort as I lie on the table of His grace. I must relax in this comfort and assurance and allow the tools of day-to-day tests and struggles to skillfully implant into my heart and mind a clearer reflection of His divine nature in me.

Prayer

Lord, I praise You and thank You that Jesus paid the price for my salvation! His precious blood covers all my sins yesterday, today, and tomorrow! I worship You for the love You shower me with— I'm worthy of Your attention only because of Your Son's sacrifice. Glory be to God! Amen.

Declaration

I am free!

Fearless

Whenever I am afraid, I will trust in You
(Psalm 56:3 NKJV).

FEAR IS AS LETHAL TO US as paralysis of the brain. It makes our thoughts become arthritic and our memory sluggish. It is the kind of feeling that can make a graceful person stumble up the stairs in a crowd. You know what I mean—the thing that makes the articulate stutter and the rhythmic become spastic. Like an oversized growth, fear soon becomes impossible to camouflage. Telltale signs like trembling knees or quivering lips betray fear even in the most disciplined person.

From the football field to the ski slope, fear has a visa or entrance that allows it to access the most discriminating crowd. It is not prejudiced, nor is it socially conscious. It can attack the impoverished or the aristocratic.

To me, there is no fear like the fear of the innocent. I can remember moments as a child when I thought my heart had turned into an African tom-tom being beaten by an insane musician whose determined efforts would soon break through my chest like the bursting of a flood-engorged dam.

Even now I can only speculate how long it took for fear to give way to normalcy or for the distant rumble of a racing heart to recede into the steadiness of practical thinking and rationality. I can't estimate time because fear traps time and holds it hostage in a prison of icy anxiety. Eventually, though, like the thawing of icicles on the roof of an aged and sagging house, my heart would gradually melt into a steady and less pronounced beat.

I confess that maturity has chased away many of the ghosts and goblins of my youthful closet of fear. Nevertheless, there are still those occasional moments when reason gives way to the fanciful imagination of the fearful little boy in me, who peeks his head out of my now fully developed frame like a turtle sticks his head out of its shell with caution and precision.

Prayer

Trusting You, Lord, is the only way to combat fear. I have been fearful at times, and only when I refocused on You rather than the cause of the fear did I find solace. May I always turn to You, Father God, to dispel fear and to take control of my mind and spirit through Your Holy Spirit. In Jesus's name, amen.

Declaration

Fear, be gone! Lord, come near!

Name Change

*Therefore God also has highly exalted Him and
given Him the name which is above every name,
that at the name of Jesus every knee should bow,
of those in heaven, and of those on earth, and of
those under the earth* (Philippians 2:9-10 NKJV).

IN THE NAME OF JESUS, you must break the spell of every
name that would attach itself to you. If your heavenly Father
didn't give you that name, then it isn't right. You are who He
says you are. Rest in the identity that He places upon you. No
one knew any better than Jacob/Israel the power of a name
change! Remember, it was in his Father's presence that he
discovered he was not a trickster but a prince!

When you believe on the covenant name of Jesus, you break
the strength of every other name that would attach itself to
your identity. In the early Church, entire cities were delivered
from satanic attack in that name. Even today, drug addicts,
lesbians, pimps, and every other name is subject to the name
of the Lord. His name is strong enough to break the bondage
of any other name that would attach itself to your life.

A good name is a very precious possession. It is often
more lucrative than financial prosperity. If your name is often
associated with wealth, ministry, scandal, etc., then your
name soon becomes synonymous with that thing. If I were
to mention certain names, you would immediately think of
Hollywood, wealth, or perhaps a certain university. Or I could

refer to other names that would immediately conjure up images of mobs, murders, adultery, or deceit.

The names of some people are damaged because of past failures and indiscretions. Still others wrestle with the stains of rumors and the disgraceful, damaging, defamation of character. Whether or not a rumor is true does not matter; people prefer excitement and speculation. The dilemma in which many people find themselves ensnared can be put like this: "How can I reverse the image or stigma that has been placed upon my name?"

Whether you have acquired an infamous name through being a victim or a villain, I have good news. If you are wrestling with the curse and stigma of public opinion, if people have categorized you for so long that you have accepted your origin for your prophecy—I still have good news for you. You don't have to stay the way you are.

Prayer

In the holy name of Jesus, I come before You, Father, humbled by Your majesty, righteousness, and faithfulness. Your name is strong enough to break every bondage of the notorious names that have attached to me over the years. Like Saul-renamed-Paul, I choose to identify with the name You assign to me, God. Thank You. In Jesus's name, amen.

Declaration

I declare my name is Child of the Living God.

God's Prevailing Opinion

*For I have come to you in my Father's name, and
you have rejected me. Yet if others come in their own
name, you gladly welcome them* (John 5:43 NLT).

THERE IS NOTHING QUITE LIKE trouble to bring out your
true identity. Aren't you glad that you are not limited to public opinion? *God's opinion will always prevail.* Those three
Hebrews came out of the furnace without a trace of smoke.
That old king tried to change the name on the package,
but he couldn't change the contents of the heart! Can you
imagine those boys shouting when they came out? One
would say, "There is none like our God!" Another would lift
his hands and say, "Jehovah is gracious!" The other would
smell his clothes, touch his hair, and shout, "Jehovah has
helped!"

If you have agonized on bended knees, praying at the
altar to know the purpose and will of God for your life, and His
answer doesn't line up with your circumstances, then call it
what God calls it! The doctor might call it cancer, but if God
calls it healed, then call it what God calls it. The Word of the
Lord often stands alone. It has no attorney and it needs no
witness. It can stand on its own merit. *Whatever He says, you
are!* If you are to fight the challenge of this age, then shake
the enemy's names and insults off your shoulder. Look the
enemy in the eye without guilt or timidity and declare:

"I have not come wearing clothes of my past. Nor will I use the opinions of this world for my defense. No, I am far wiser through the things I have suffered. Therefore, I have come in my Father's name. He has anointed my head, counseled my fears, and taught me who I am. I am covered by His anointing, comforted by His presence, and kept by His auspicious grace. Today, as never before, I stand in the identity He has given me and renounce every memory of who I was yesterday. I was called for such a time as this, and I have come in my Father's name!"

Prayer

Father God, Your opinion is the only one that matters—I will lean into what You say about this and that in my life. Your authority and power and anointing are all I need to have a blessed and abundant life, knowing Your provision is enough. Always enough. In Jesus's name, amen.

Declaration

I come in my Father's name. I know who I am and *whose* I am!

Unity

There is neither Jew nor Greek, there is neither slave nor free, there is neither male nor female; for you are all one in Christ Jesus (Galatians 3:28 NKJV).

SOME OF US HAVE particular problems based on where we came from. And we have to deal with it. God says there is neither Greek nor Jew. There is no such thing as a Black church. There is no such thing as a White church. It's only one Church, purchased by the blood of the Lamb. We are all one in Christ Jesus. You may have been born with a silver spoon in your mouth, but it doesn't make any difference. In the Kingdom of God, social status doesn't mean anything. Rahab can be mentioned right next to Sarah because if you believe, God will bless. Faith is the only thing in this world where there is true equal opportunity. Everyone can come to Jesus.

God doesn't look at your gender. He looks at your heart. He doesn't look at morality and good works. He looks at the faith that lives within. God is looking in your heart. You are spirit and spirits are sexless. That's why angels don't have sexes; they simply are ministering spirits. Don't think of angels in terms of gender. They can manifest themselves as men, but angels are really ministering spirits. All people are one in Christ Jesus.

> *Therefore, having been justified by faith, we have peace with God through our Lord Jesus Christ,*

through whom also we have access by faith into
this grace in which we stand, and rejoice in hope
of the glory of God (Romans 5:1-2 NKJV).

Christ saw the worth of the infirm woman of Luke 13 because she was a daughter of Abraham. She had faith. He will unleash you also from the pain you have struggled with and the frustrations that have plagued you. Faith is truly equal opportunity. If you will but dare to believe that you are a daughter or son of Abraham, you will find the power to stand up straight and be unleashed. The potential that has been bound will then truly be set free.

Prayer

In the name of Jesus, I believe that the true Church welcomes all people—knowing that You, Lord God, love each person as Your child. As Your Word says in 2 Peter 3:9 (NIV), *"The Lord is not slow in keeping his promise, as some understand slowness. Instead he is patient with you,* **not wanting anyone to perish, but everyone to come** *to repentance."* Amen.

Declaration

Faith truly offers equal opportunity for all!

Encouragement

Because God wanted to make the unchanging nature of his purpose very clear to the heirs of what was promised, he confirmed it with an oath. God did this so that, by two unchangeable things in which it is impossible for God to lie, we who have fled to take hold of the hope set before us may be greatly encouraged (Hebrews 6:17-18 NIV).

REACH OUT AND EMBRACE the fact that God has been watching over you all of your life. He covers you, He clothes you, and He blesses you! Rejoice in Him in spite of the broken places. God's grace is sufficient for your needs and your scars. He will anoint you with oil. The anointing of the Lord be upon you now! May it bathe, heal, and strengthen you as never before.

> *When he arrived and saw what the grace of God had done, he was glad and encouraged them all to remain true to the Lord with all their hearts* (Acts 11:23 NIV).

For the hurting, God has intensive care. There will be times in your life when God nurtures you through crisis situations. You may not even realize how many times God has intervened to relieve the tensions and stresses of day-to-day living. Every now and then He does us a favor. Yes, a favor: something we didn't earn or can't even explain, except as the loving hand of

God. He knows when the load is overwhelming. Many times He moves (it seems to us) just in the nick of time.

> *May the God who gives endurance and encouragement give you the same attitude of mind toward each other that Christ Jesus had* (Romans 15:5 NIV).

God is constantly reassuring us that we might have a consolation and a hope for the soul, the mind and emotions, steadfast and unmovable. He gives us security and assurance.

> *You, Lord, hear the desire of the afflicted; you encourage them, and you listen to their cry* (Psalm 10:17 NIV).

Prayer

Heavenly Father, I come to You in the name of Jesus, praising and thanking You for nurturing me through every crisis situation—whether I know You've intervened or not. Your encouragement comes in so many ways—just when I need it, You're there for me. Most gratefully, and in Jesus's name, amen.

Declaration

God's grace and encouragement will carry me through every crisis.

Power

*Hereafter the Son of Man will sit on the right
hand of the power of God* (Luke 22:69 NKJV).

*You are worthy, O Lord, to receive glory and honor
and power; for You created all things, and by Your will
they exist and were created* (Revelation 4:11 NKJV).

ONLY WHEN WE ARE weary from trying to unlock our own resources do we come to the Lord, receive Him, and *allow Him to release in us the power to become* whatever we need to be. Actually, isn't that what we want to know—our purpose? Then we can use the power to become who we really are. Life has chiseled many of us into mere fragments of who we were meant to be. To all who receive Him, Christ gives the power to slip out of who they were forced into being, so they can transform into the individual they each were created to be.

Salvation as it relates to destiny is the God-given power to become what He has eternally decreed you were before. "Before what?" you ask. Before the foundation of the world. What Christians so often refer to as grace truly is God's divine enablement to accomplish predestined purpose. When the Lord says to Paul, *"My grace is sufficient for you"* (2 Corinthians 12:9 NKJV), He is simply stating that His power is not intimidated by your circumstances. *You are empowered by*

God to reach and accomplish goals that transcend human limitations! It is important for each and every vessel God uses to realize that they were able to accomplish what others could not only because God gave them the grace to do so. Problems are not really problems to a person who has the grace to serve in a particular area.

How many times have people walked up to me and said, "I don't see how you can stand this or that." If God has given us the grace to operate in a certain situation, those things do not affect us as they would someone else who does not have the grace to function in that area. Therefore, it is important that we not imitate other people. Assuming that we may be equally talented, we still may not be equally graced. Remember, God always empowers whomever He employs.

Ultimately, we must realize that the excellency of our gifts is of God and not of us. He doesn't need nearly as much of our contributions as we think He does. So it is God who works out our internal destinies. He gives us the power to become who we are eternally and internally.

Prayer

Christ Jesus, thank You for giving me the power to slip out of who I was forced into being, so I can transform into the individual I was created to be. I gladly accept Your divine enablement to accomplish my predestined purpose. Use me, Lord, for Your will to be done on earth as it is in Heaven. In Jesus's name, amen.

Declaration

God's power is not intimidated by my circumstances.

Repentance

*Him God has exalted to His right hand to be
Prince and Savior, to give repentance to Israel
and forgiveness of sins* (Acts 5:31 NKJV).

CHANGE IS A GIFT FROM GOD. It is given to those who
are too far removed from what they feel destiny has ordained
for them. There is nothing wrong with being wrong—but
there is something wrong with not making the necessary
adjustments to get things right! Even within the Christian
community, some do not believe in God's ability to change
the human heart. This unbelief in God's ability causes people to judge others on the basis of their past. Dead issues are
periodically revived in the mouths of gossips. Still, the Lord
progressively regenerates the mind of His children. Don't
assume that real change occurs without struggle and prayer.
However, change can be achieved.

The Bible calls change repentance. Repentance is God's
gift to struggling hearts. The Lord wants to bring you to a
place of safety and shelter. Without the Holy Spirit's help, you
can search and search and still not find repentance. The Lord
will show the place of repentance only to those who hunger
and thirst after righteousness.

One moment with the Spirit of God can lead you into a
place of renewal that, on your own, you would not find
or enjoy. I believe it was this kind of grace that made John
Newton write these lines in the song "Amazing Grace":

"'Twas grace that taught my heart to fear, and grace my fears relieved; how precious did that grace appear the hour I first believed." When God gives you the grace to make changes that you know you couldn't do in your own strength, His grace becomes precious to you.

Prayer

Spirit of God, I never thought of repentance as a gift from You—but of course it is because all good things are from You! I pray that You will show me the place of repentance as I truly hunger and thirst after Your righteousness. In Jesus's name, amen.

Declaration

I want to get things right!

Good Friends

*And we know that all things work together for good
to those who love God, to those who are the called
according to His purpose* (Romans 8:28 NKJV).

IF NO GOOD CAN COME out of a relationship or situation,
then God will not allow it. This knowledge sets us free from
internal struggle and allows us to be transparent. *"Every
good and perfect gift is from above, coming down from the
Father of the heavenly lights, who does not change like shifting shadows"* (James 1:17 NIV). If you don't understand the
sovereignty of God, then all is lost. There must be an inner
awareness within your heart, a deep knowledge that God is
in control and that He is able to reverse the adverse. When we
believe in His sovereignty, we can overcome every humanly
induced trial because we realize that it is divinely permitted
and supernaturally orchestrated. He orchestrates them in
such a way that the things that could have paralyzed us only
motivate us.

God delights in bestowing His abundant grace upon us
so we can live without fear. In Christ, we come to the table
of human relationships feeling like we are standing before
a great "smorgasbord" or buffet table. There will be some
relationships whose "taste" we prefer over others, but the
richness of life is in the opportunity to explore the options.
What a dull plate we would face if everything on it was

duplicated without distinction. God creates different types of people, and all are His handiwork.

Even in the most harmonious of relationships there are injuries and adversity. If you live in a cocoon, you will miss all the different levels of love God has for you. God allows different people to come into your life to accomplish His purposes. Your friends are ultimately the ones who will help you become all that God wants you to be in Him. When you consider it in that light, you have many friends—some of them expressed friends and some implied friends.

Prayer

Dear Best Friend, I am in awe of Your attention to every detail in my life, including my relationships with friends. Thank You for my BFFs and for my casual friends and for the friends I've yet to meet. *"When Jesus saw their faith, he said, 'Friend, your sins are forgiven'"* (Luke 5:20 NIV). You are my very best Friend forever and eternally. In Your name I pray, amen.

Declaration

Jesus is my Friend. In Him I have my being.

Understanding

Joyful is the person who finds wisdom, the one who gains understanding (Proverbs 3:13 NLT).

WHEN WE EXPERIENCE the new birth, we again go back to the formative years of being deeply impressionable. It's important to be discerning in who we allow to influence us in the early years. Whenever we become intimate with someone, the first thing we should want to know is, "Who do you say that I am?" Our basic need is to be understood by the inner circle of people with whom we walk.

However, we must be ready to abort negative, destructive information that doesn't bring us into an accelerated awareness of inner realities and strengths. Jesus was able to ask Peter, "Who do you say that I am?" because He already knew the answer! (See Matthew 16:15.) To ask someone to define you without first knowing the answer within yourself is dangerous. When we ask that kind of question, without an inner awareness, we open the door for manipulation. In short, Jesus knew who He was.

The Lord wants to help you realize who you are and what you are graced to do. When you understand that He is the only One who really knows you, then you pursue Him with fierceness and determination. Pursue Him! Listen to what the apostle Paul shares at the meeting on Mars Hill:

From one man he [God] created all the nations throughout the whole earth. He decided before-hand when they should rise and fall, and he determined their boundaries. His purpose was for the nations to seek after God and perhaps feel their way toward him and find him—though he is not far from any one of us. For in him we live and move and exist. As some of your own poets have said, "We are his offspring" (Acts 17:26-28 NLT).

The basic message of this passage is that God has set the bounds on our habitations. He knows who we are and how we are to find Him. This knowledge, locked up in the counsel of God's omniscience, is the basis of our pursuit, our understanding, and it is the release of that knowledge that brings immediate transformation. He knows the hope or the goal of our calling. He is not far removed from us; He reveals Himself to people who seek Him. The finders are the seekers. The door is opened only to the knockers, and the gifts are given to the askers! (See Luke 11:9.) Initiation is our responsibility. Whosoever hungers and thirsts shall be filled. Remember, in every crisis He is never far from the seeker!

Prayer

Father God, may I always seek You, searching for understanding and every knowledge You want to gift me with. I will seek and knock, hunger and thirst until You fill me to overflowing with Your love, counsel, and wisdom. In the name of Your Son, Jesus, amen.

Declaration

I am defined by God's definition!

Compassion

Through the Lord's mercies we are not consumed, because His compassions fail not. They are new every morning; great is Your faithfulness (Lamentations 3:22-23 NKJV).

"FORGIVE ME FOR CONDEMNING and judging anybody else. I know that if it were not for Your mercy, I would be guilty of the very things for which I have disdained others. Help me not to be hypocritical." This kind of prayer and confession enhances your relationship with God as you begin to realize that you *were* saved by grace, you *are* saved by grace, and you *will be* saved by grace! Knowing this, how can you not be grateful?

You know that God loves you so much that He stays in the house you haven't fully cleaned. He hates the acts and despises the thoughts, but He loves the thinker.

> *Nothing in all creation is hidden from God. Everything is naked and exposed before his eyes, and he is the one to whom we are accountable. So then, since we have a great High Priest who has entered heaven, Jesus the Son of God, let us hold firmly to what we believe. This High Priest of ours understands our weaknesses, for he faced all of the same testings we do, yet he did not sin* (Hebrews 4:13-15 NLT).

Immediately after the writer of the book of Hebrews tells us that God knows all our business and that all our thoughts parade around naked before His scrutinizing eyes, he mentions the High Priest that we have in Christ. He knows we are going to need a high priest for all the garbage and information that the Holy Spirit is privy to, yet others would never know. What greater compassion can be displayed than when the writer goes on to say that God, through Christ, can be *touched by how I feel*. No wonder Jeremiah said His mercies are "new every morning"! (See Lamentations 3:22-23.)

Prayer

Lord, may You grant me the compassion of Jesus: "*When he saw the crowds, he had compassion on them because they were confused and helpless, like sheep without a shepherd.*" (Matthew 9:36 NLT) May I have the opportunity to share Your Good News with people You place in my path. In Jesus's name, amen.

Declaration

I am saved by His grace and compassion—hallelujah!

Enrichment

*Now may He who supplies seed to the sower, and bread for food, supply and multiply the seed you have sown and increase the fruits of your righteousness, while **you are enriched in everything** for all liberality, which causes thanksgiving through us to God* (2 Corinthians 9:10-11 NKJV).

IF IN YOUR THOUGHTS you see something beyond where you are, if you see a dream, a goal, or an aspiration that others would think impossible, you may have to *hold it.* Sometimes you may have to *hide it,* and most of the time you will have to *water it* as a farmer waters his crops to sustain the life in them. But always remember they are your fields. You must eat from the garden of your own thoughts, so don't grow anything you don't want to eat.

As you ponder and daydream, receive grace for the hard places and healing for the damaged soil. Just know that whenever your children, your friends, or anyone else comes to the table of your wisdom, you can only feed them what you have grown in your own fields. Your wisdom is so flavorful and its texture so rich that it can't be "store bought"—it must be homegrown.

A whispering prayer lies on my lips: *I pray that this word God has given me be so powerful and personal, so intimate and applicable, that it leaves behind it a barren mind made pregnant. This seed of greatness will explode in your life and harvest in your children, feeding the generations to come and changing the winds of destiny.*

As I move on to other issues and as we face our inner selves, we strip away our facades and see ourselves as we really are. I am not fearful of our nakedness nor discouraged by our flaws. In my heart I smell the indescribable smell of an approaching rain. Moisture is in the air, and the clouds have gathered. Our fields have been chosen for the next rain, and the wind has already started to blow.

Run swiftly into the field with your precious seeds, and plant them in the soft ground of your fertile mind. Whatever you plant in the evening will be reaped in the morning. My friend, I am so excited for you. I just heard a clap of thunder... in just another moment, there'll be rain!

Prayer

My Creator, knowing that I must eat from the garden of my own thoughts, as I ponder and daydream, I ask for Your grace for the hard places and healing for the damaged soil in my life. May You help me plant the seeds that will yield an abundantly fruitful future. Thank You. In Jesus's name, amen.

Declaration

I am not fearful or discouraged! I feel God's nourishing and refreshing rain on my face!

Restoration

*Restore us, Lord God Almighty; make your
face shine on us* (Psalm 80:19 NIV).

DEAD CIRCUMSTANCES CANNOT hold down the body of someone who has been chosen! If no one else embraces these bleeding, Purple Heart soldiers, perhaps they should rally together and find comfort in the commonality of their mutual experience. Thank God for Jephthah, who reminds us of the deep, abiding reality that even if we were thrown into a refuse receptacle by closed minds who decided that our dry bones couldn't live again, God is still in the business of recycling human lives!

I must confess that more than once I have seen His hand pick up the pieces of this broken heart and restore back to service my crushed emotions and murky confidence, while I stood in awe at the fact that God can do so much with so little.

The greatest place to preach isn't in our large meetings with swelling crowds and lofty recognitions. The greatest place to preach is in the trenches, in the foxholes and the hog pens of life. If you want a grateful audience, take your message to the messy places of life, and scrape the hog hairs off the prodigal sons of God, who were locked away in the hog pens by the spiritual elite.

In these abominable situations, you will find true worship being born, springing out of the hearts of those who realize the riches of His grace. No worship seminar is needed for someone whose tearstained face has turned from humiliation to inspiration. Their personal degradation has become a living demonstration of the depths of the unfathomable love of God!

My friend, this is Davidic worship! This is the praise of David, whose critical brothers and distracted father helped him become the canvas on which God paints the finest picture of worship these weary eyes have ever witnessed! It is time for us to redefine and redirect our gaze to find the heroes of God among us. We must not forget that God purposely chooses to restore and use misplaced and rejected people—and He may be looking in our direction.

Prayer

Lord God Almighty, restoration is all part of my salvation—restoring the bond between You and me through the sacrifice of Your Son on the Cross. Oh, how eternally grateful I am that He chose to be beaten and scorned and murdered, all to restore our relationship with You. In humble adoration and in His name I pray, amen.

Declaration

I am redeemed and restored, in Jesus's name!

Crowns

The twenty-four elders fall down before Him who sits on the throne and worship Him who lives forever and ever, and cast their crowns before the throne, saying: "You are worthy, O Lord, to receive glory and honor and power; for You created all things, and by Your will they exist and were created" (Revelation 4:10-11 NKJV).

THERE IS A PLACE in the presence of God where crowns lose their luster. There is a place where human accolades sound brash and out of pitch. There is a place where all our memorials of great accomplishments seem like dusty stones gathered by bored children who had nothing better to collect. There are times when we trade success for solace.

In the book of Revelation, 24 elders traded their golden, jewel-encrusted crowns for a tearstained moment in the presence of a bloodstained Lamb. Many wonderful people are suffering with their success because they cannot discern when to throw down their crowns and just worship.

I drove a delivery truck one summer while I was in college. I had never driven a stick shift before. It was all right at first. I handled it rather well. In fact, I was on my way to that special place of self-enthroned egotism when I had to stop at a traffic light. The only problem was, this light was on a steep hill. I had to keep my left foot on the clutch while easing my right foot from the brake to the gas with the timing and grace of Fred Astaire. My first attempt caused the truck to lurch forward. Then the engine died, and the whole truck started sliding backward. I nearly slid into a car that was behind me. I was sick! Traffic was backing up, and I could see the person in my rearview mirror saying something that I was glad I couldn't quite hear!

I finally prayed—which is what I should have done first. My task was getting the timing. I had to learn when to ease my right foot off the brake and onto the gas and my left foot from the clutch with computerlike precision without killing the engine. When it was all over, my head was spinning, my pulse was weak, and (to be blunt) my bladder was full! In spite of all that, I learned something on that hill that many people don't learn about themselves and the things they hold on to. I learned when to let go!

Prayer

Lord, a good lesson to learn is when to let go of things (and even people) that cause a traffic jam in my life. May my praise and worship and seeking Your will for my life be front and center on the road You lead me to. Any crowns I may have accumulated along the way will be placed before You as a small token of my love for You. In Jesus's name, amen.

Declaration

**God is worthy to receive all glory
and honor and power!**

Exposure

Wearing a linen ephod, David was dancing before the Lord with all his might, while he and all Israel were bringing up the ark of the Lord with shouts and the sound of trumpets. As the ark of the Lord was entering the City of David, Michal daughter of Saul watched from a window. And when she saw King David leaping and dancing before the Lord, she despised him in her heart (2 Samuel 6:14-16 NIV).

BY GOD'S DESIGN, left splayed before us on the pages of the Scriptures are the intricate details of the life of David, whose passions were both an asset and a liability. We filter through his secret thoughts as casually as if we were reading the evening newspaper. His inner struggles and childhood dysfunctions are openly aired on the pages of the text like the center foldout in a tabloid.

God didn't display David's failures in a divine attempt to expose the secret prayers of His struggling king. Rather, God's purpose is to give us a point of reference that exhibits His manifold grace. How marvelous is the message that instructs us that if God could use a David, He also can use us, as we are all people of *like passions.*

I do not dispute the passions. In fact, without them I can never migrate from the obscure hills and shepherd fields of yesteryear to the victorious acquisition of the palace to which I have been called. Yet I want to issue a point of warning in the midst of this dissertation to the ones who dare to lay bare their innermost passions and desires before God—He who has examined the inner workings of every heart.

Did you know that God used people who were similarly affected (as you are) by certain stimuli and struggles? What a joy to know that treasure can be surrounded by trash and still not lose its value! Is a diamond less valuable if it is found in a clogged drain? Of course not!

Prayer

Like David, Lord, my struggles at times are many, and my enemies surround me—yet also like David, I will turn to You to find solace and forgiveness and peace. You are the light in a dark world, and I will continue to walk toward Your brilliant rays of life. I offer You this prayer in Jesus's name. Amen.

Declaration

I strive to be a child after God's own heart!

Awakening to Reality

It was time for supper, and the devil had already prompted Judas, son of Simon Iscariot, to betray Jesus. Jesus knew that the Father had given him authority over everything and that he had come from God and would return to God. So he got up from the table, took off his robe, wrapped a towel around his waist, and poured water into a basin. Then he began to wash the disciples' feet, drying them with the towel he had around him (John 13:2-5 NLT).

SUPPER IS OVER and the dishes are cleared away. Supper is also over for those of us who have had a "reality check" through the unveiling of Judas. We now realize that our ultimate purpose for gathering isn't really for fellowship.

God gathers us to sharpen and prune us through our attempts at fellowship. He often uses the people with whom we worship to prune us. They become the utensils the Lord uses to perfect those whom He has called. As lavishly garnished as the table is, and as decorative as it may appear to the youthful gaze of the new Christian, it is only a matter of time before they begin the stage-by-stage unmasking and realize that the guests around the table of the Lord are bleeding.

Imagine how shocked you would be to find yourself invited to a prestigious dinner party like this one. You have been so careful to respond appropriately. Now showered and manicured, clean and perfumed, you carefully begin the laborious task of attiring yourself in an elegant, yet tasteful manner. You desperately want to make a positive impression on the Host, as well as on the guests. After arriving on time, you hasten toward the door, where you are announced and then ushered into the banqueting room of your dreams.

As your eyes begin to warily make the rounds across the table, a bitter taste of bile begins to rise and lodge in your throat. Each guest has some sort of gross deformity beneath their gracious smile. Neither rubies nor diamonds, neither tuxedos nor tails can camouflage the scars and gaping wounds represented around the table. You are shocked that you spent all evening trying to prepare yourself to meet people who have more flaws than you have ever imagined! The only spotless splendor for the human eye to gaze upon is the Host Himself—all others are merely patients: just mutilated, torn, dilapidated, disfigured caricatures of social grace and ambiance.

Prayer

I admit, Father, that I would rather wear rose-colored glasses than see clearly the flaws and failures of fellow Christians. I pray that You would give me Your perspective and Your love to see people according to Your will. Soften my gaze, Lord, to realize that I, too, am in need of sharpening and pruning, and may I welcome the change. In my Savior's name, amen.

Declaration

I will gracefully and purposely dine with whomever the Lord seats at my table.

Humbleness

But among you it will be different. Whoever wants to be a leader among you must be your servant, and whoever wants to be first among you must become your slave. For even the Son of Man came not to be served but to serve others and to give his life as a ransom for many (Matthew 20:26-28 NLT).

WAILING, SHRIEKS OF BROKEN HEARTS, and screams of terror echo behind our stiffly starched shirts and satiny-smooth dresses. The words have increased and the technology has improved, but the power of ministry will never be unleashed until those who are called to deliver it find the grace, or perhaps the mercy, that will allow them to *lay aside their garments!*

"Is He mad? Has He lost His mind?" Can you imagine what the disciples thought as Jesus changed the atmosphere of the feast by disrobing before them? How could a person of His stature stoop so low? I tell you, He never stood as tall as He did when He stooped so low to bless the men whom He had taught. Even Peter said, *"Lord, not my feet only, but also my hands and my head"* (John 13:9 NKJV).

We are still squirming and fuming over exposing, forgiving, and washing one another's feet! We need the whole of us cleansed! We have never accepted people in the Church. We take in numbers and teach them to project an image, but we have never allowed people—real people—to find a place at our table!

Jesus was running out of time. He had no more time for fun and games. He ended the supper and laid aside His garments. Hear me, my friend; we, too, are running out of time! We have a generation before us that has not been moved by our lavish banquets or by the glamorous buildings we have built.

Someone, quick! Call the supper to an end, and tell us who you really are beneath your churchy look and your pious posture. Tell us something that makes us comfortable with our own nudity. We have carefully hidden our struggles and paraded only our victories, but the whole country is falling asleep at the parade!

Prayer

I wonder how I would react at the supper seeing Jesus acting like a servant. Would I, like the majority of the disciples, become indignant, or would I be like impetuous Peter and want Him to wash me whole? Lord, now, today, I know Your Son has indeed washed me whole with His blood shed at Calvary. Glory to God and amen!

Declaration

I will stoop as low as Jesus to serve Him and bring in the Kingdom harvest.

Bareness

*For by the grace given me I say to every one
of you: Do not think of yourself more highly
than you ought, but rather think of yourself
with sober judgment, in accordance with the
faith God has distributed to each of you. For
just as each of us has one body with many
members, and these members do not all have
the same function* (Romans 12:3-4 NIV).

THANK GOD FOR ALL THE Kathryn Kuhlmans, the Oral
Roberts, and others whose lives have touched the world.
The hot blaze of camera lights never caught the true basis of
their ministries. It was the things they laid aside that made
them who they were. Thank God they laid them aside. Thousands were healed because they did. Thousands were saved
because they did.

What about "Pastor Littlechurch" and "Evangelist Nobody"
who never sold a tape or wrote a book? They paid the price
nonetheless, and for the souls they touched they are unsung
heroes. Like Noah, their membership roll never exceeded
eight souls, but they faithfully led them. They wanted to do
more. They thought they would go further than they did,
but they had laid aside their garments. They said, "If I am not
called to help everybody, then please, God, let me help somebody!" This is the cost of Christianity stripped down to one
desire, stripped to the simplicity of bareness.

The truth of the matter is that when we are stripped bare, there is no difference between the executive and the janitor. When we are stripped bare, there is no difference between the usher and the pastor. Is that why we are afraid to let anyone see who we really are? Have we become so addicted to our distinctions that we have lost our commonality?

There are no differences in the feet of the washed and the feet of the one who washes them. Your ministry truly becomes effective when you know that there is precious little difference between the people you serve and yourself. Then and only then have you laid aside your garments!

Marriages are failing across the country because couples are reciting vows before an overworked preacher, and an overspent family, promising to do what they will never be able to do! Why? You can't love anybody like that until you lay aside your garments and allow their needs to supersede your needs. They can never be one until they have laid aside their garments. Then and only then can they come together as one.

Prayer

In the name of Jesus and by the grace given to me by God, I will not think of myself more highly than I should. Lord, with the help of the Holy Spirit, I will think of myself with sober judgment and willingly lay aside my garments in accordance with the faith You have gifted me. Amen.

Declaration

God, use me as You see fit to advance Your Kingdom on earth as it is in Heaven.

Seasons

Let us not grow weary while doing good, for in due season we shall reap if we do not lose heart (Galatians 6:9 NKJV).

DO YOU REMEMBER how in winter icicles hung from the roofs of old houses, pointing toward the ground like stalactites in a cave? As the cold blitz of winter was challenged by budding trees and warmer days, the icicles began to drip and diminish. Slowly the earth changed its clothes for a new season.

Winter is just the prelude God plays to introduce the concerto of summer. In spite of its cold, frostbitten hand seizing our forest, lawns, and streams, its grip can still be broken through the patient perseverance of the season that is sensitive to timing and divine purpose.

There is nothing like a sense of time. It cannot be faked. It is like seeing a choir sway to the beat of a gospel ballad. Someone invariably will be moving spastically, trying desperately to simulate a sense of timing. Moving his feet with all the grace of the Tin Man in "The Wizard of Oz," he can't quite learn what the body has to sense. The lack of timing is as detrimental as planting corn in the bitter winds of an Alaskan winter. There may be absolutely nothing wrong with the seed or the ground, just the time the farmer chose to expect the process to occur.

Assuming that you understand the necessity of small beginnings, and assuming that you realize whatever you have will not replace the One who gave it and that success only creates a platform for responsibility to be enlarged—then you can begin to ascertain where you are on the calendar, the divine almanac of God. Did you know that God has an almanac? Perhaps you do not know what an almanac is. My mother always consulted the almanac to determine the best time to plant the crop she intended to harvest. It is a calendar that presents the seasons and cycles of a year. You see, the principle of seed time and harvest will not override the understanding of time and purpose. God does everything according to His eternal almanac of time and purpose!

Prayer

Heavenly Father, may I always be in season with You, in step with Your time and purpose. May I not lose heart while working to help bring in Your harvest. In the mighty name of Jesus, amen.

Declaration

**I will not grow weary while doing
God's good in the world.**

Wholeness

[Christ] *who being the brightness of His glory and the express image of His person, and upholding all things by the word of His power, when He had by Himself purged our sins, sat down at the right hand of the Majesty on high* (Hebrews 1:3 NKJV).

I WANT TO ZOOM IN on the Sabbath day because what the Sabbath was physically, Christ is spiritually. Christ is our Sabbath rest. He is the end of our labors. We are saved by grace through faith and not by works, lest anyone should be able to boast (see Ephesians 2:8-9). Jesus says, *"Come to Me, all you who labor and are heavy laden, and I will give you rest. Take My yoke upon you and learn from Me, for I am gentle and lowly in heart, and you will find rest for your souls. For My yoke is easy and My burden is light"* (Matthew 11:28-30 NKJV).

The rest of the Lord is so complete that when Jesus was dying on the Cross, He said, *"It is finished"* (John 19:30). It was so powerful. For the first time in history, a high priest sat down in the presence of God without having to run in and out bringing blood to atone for sin. When Christ entered in once and for all, He offered up Himself for us that we might be delivered from sin, that we would receive wholeness.

If you really want to be healed, you've got to be in Him. If you really want to be set free and experience restoration, you've got to be in Him, because your healing comes in the Sabbath rest. Your wholeness comes in Christ Jesus. As you rest in Him, every infirmity, every area bent out of place will be restored.

The devil knows this truth, so he does not want you to rest in the Lord. Satan wants you to be anxious. He wants you to be upset. He wants you to be hysterical. He wants you to be suicidal, doubtful, fearful, and neurotic. Destroy evil plots and temptations with God's Word—as Jesus did in the wilderness, you can too!

Prayer

When Christ offered Himself for me, I received wholeness and healing, Lord. I thank You that I have been set free and have experienced restoration. As I rest in You, my spiritual, physical, and mental health is restored—I claim this promise in Jesus's name. Amen.

Declaration

**I am healthy in body, mind, and soul
because of Jesus's sacrifice!**

Family

Now all of us can come to the Father through the same Holy Spirit because of what Christ has done for us. So now you Gentiles are no longer strangers and foreigners. You are citizens along with all of God's holy people. You are members of God's family (Ephesians 2:18-19 NLT).

THERE IS A DEVILISH PREJUDICE in the Church that denies the blood to its uncomely members. If a person has a failure in an area we relate to because we have a similar weakness, we immediately praise God for the blood that cleanses us from all unrighteousness. If they are unfortunate enough to fail where we are very strong, then we condemn them. We tie a string around those members to mark them, and we deny them the blood.

The spirit of Cain is loose in the Church! We have spilled our brother's blood because he is different, because his skin or his sin is different from ours. Untie them right now, in the name of the Lord, and restore to them the opportunity to experience the life that only comes to the flesh through the blood. Without the blood all flesh dies—Black, White, rich, poor, homosexual, heterosexual, drug addict, or alcoholic. Without the blood of Christ to save it and the Holy Spirit to empower it, no flesh can be saved.

But by the blood of the Lamb, anyone, regardless of their failures or past sins, can come equally and unashamedly to the foot of the Cross and allow the drops of Jesus's blood to invigorate the soul that sin has lacerated and destroyed. We will never experience massive revival until we allow all sinners to come to the fountain filled with blood, drawn from Emmanuel's veins!

Have you ever been guilty of having a condescending attitude about another person's weakness? I am ashamed to admit it, but I have. How can we dare to think we can access the soul-cleansing blood that delivers us from the cesspool of our secret sins—and then look down on another member of Christ's body in disdain? How can we forbid them access to the only answer to the massive problems that consume our generation?

Prayer

Lord God, please forgive me for the times I have judged people for their past sins or failures. This is not Your way or will for my life—I must not have a condescending or judgmental attitude about any of Your children. I must love them as You love them—give me the wisdom and compassion to do so. In Jesus's name, amen.

Declaration

I will treat others as I desire them to treat me.

Belonging

So we praise God for the glorious grace he has poured out on us who belong to his dear Son (Ephesians 1:6 NLT).

I REMEMBER, in my early days as a new Christian, that I tried to become what I thought all the other Christians were. I didn't understand that my goal should have been to achieve God's purpose for my life. I was young and so impressionable. Secretly suffering from low self-esteem, I thought that the Christians around me had mastered a level of holiness that seemed to evade me. I groaned in the night; I cried out to God to create in me a robotlike piety that would satisfy what I thought was required of me. I deeply admired those virtuous "faith heroes" whose flowery testimonies loftily hung around the ceiling like steam gathering above a shower. They seemed so changed, so sure, and so stable! I admired their standards and their purity, and I earnestly prayed, *Make me better, Lord!*

I don't think I have changed that prayer, but I have changed the *motivation* behind it. Suddenly, I began to realize that God knew me and loved me as I was, although I had never been taught about perfect love. I had always been surrounded by a love that was based upon performance. So I thought God's love was doled out according to a merit system. If I did well today, God loved me. However, if I failed, He did not love me. What a roller-coaster ride! I didn't know from moment to moment whether I was accepted in the beloved—or not!

I viewed my friends as paragons, or ultimate examples of what I should be, and I attacked my carnality with brutality. I didn't realize that everything that is born has to grow and develop to maturity. I was expecting an immediate, powerful, all-inclusive metamorphosis that would transform me into a new creature of perfection. Granted, I had never realized this goal, but I was also sure it was possible—and that this perfect creature must be much better than I. Surely God was waiting on him to come forth, so He could *really* love me.

Prayer

Dear God, make me better at loving You and those around me. Make me better at giving You praise in every circumstance. Make me better at giving You all the glory and honor. God, make me better at fulfilling Your will in my life. In Jesus's name, amen.

Declaration

I believe in and belong to God the Father, Jesus the Son, and the Holy Spirit.

Stillness

*Be still, and know that I am God; I will be
exalted among the nations, I will be exalted
in the earth!* (Psalm 46:10 NKJV).

ALL TOO OFTEN, our thoughts and conversations reveal
that we wrestle with characters who have moved on and
events that don't really matter. The people who surround us
are kept on hold while we invest massive amounts of attention to areas of the past that are dead and possess no ability
to reward. It is like slow dancing alone or singing harmony
when there is no melody. There is something missing that
causes our presentation to lose its luster. Stop the music!
Your partner is gone, and you are waiting by yourself!

I think the greatest of all depressions comes when we live
and gather our successes just *to prove something to someone who isn't even looking.* The problem is, we can't really
appreciate our successes because they are done *by us* but
not *for us.* They are done in the name of a person, place, or
thing that has moved on, leaving us trapped in a time warp,
wondering why we aren't fulfilled by our job, ministry, or
good fortune.

God did most of His work on creation with no one around
to applaud His accomplishments. So He praised Himself. He
said, "It is good!" Have you stopped to appreciate what God
has allowed you to accomplish, or have you been too busy
trying to make an impression on someone? No one paints

for the blind or sings for the deaf. Their level of appreciation is hindered by their physical limitations. Although they may be fine connoisseurs in some other arena, they will never appreciate what they can't detect.

Let's clap and cheer for the people whose absence teaches us the gift of being alone. Somewhere beyond loneliness there is contentment, and contentment is born out of necessity. It springs up in the hum of the heart that lives in an empty house—and in the smirk and smile that come on the faces of those who have amused themselves with their own thoughts.

Prayer

Oh Lord, You know how many times I have "performed" for people who don't even care about the performance or aren't even part of my life anymore. Oh, what futile efforts I make when I could be devoting precious time to Your purpose. Please forgive me, and make me aware of those wasteful times with a nudge from the Holy Spirit. In Jesus's name, amen.

Declaration

I will stop gathering successes just to prove something to someone who doesn't even care.

Worship

*Give unto the Lord the glory due to His name; **worship** the Lord in the beauty of holiness* (Psalm 29:2 NKJV).

*And when they had come into the house, they saw the young Child with Mary His mother, and fell down and **worshiped** Him. And when they had opened their treasures, they presented gifts to Him: gold, frankincense, and myrrh* (Matthew 2:11 NKJV).

*Then Jesus said to him, "Away with you, Satan! For it is written, 'You shall **worship** the Lord your God, and Him only you shall serve'"* (Matthew 4:10 NKJV).

IN THE SPECIAL MOMENTS when thankful hearts and hands lifted in praise come into corporate levels of expression, with memories of what could have happened had God not intervened, we find our real ministry. Above all titles and professions, every Christian is called to be a *worshipper*. We are a royal priesthood that might have become extinct had the mercy of the Lord not arrested the villainous horrors of the enemy. Calloused hands are raised in praise—hands that tell a story of struggle, whether spiritual or natural.

By him therefore let us offer the sacrifice of praise to God continually, that is, the fruit of our lips giving thanks to his name (Hebrews 13:15 KJV).

God is Spirit, and those who worship Him must worship in spirit and truth (John 4:24 NKJV).

But the hour is coming, and now is, when the true worshipers will worship the Father in spirit and truth; for the Father is seeking such to worship Him (John 4:23 NKJV).

The intensity of our praise is born out of the ever-freshness of our memories, not so much of our past but of His mercies toward us. The issue then is not whether we remember—but how we choose to remember what we've been through. He is able to take the sting out of the memory and still leave the sweet taste of victory intact. When that happens, we are enriched by our struggles, not limited. Lift up your head and be blessed in the presence of the Lord. Nothing is nearly as important as worshipping the Lord. What if all the voices on earth harmoniously exploded into accolades of appreciation for God's majesty, honor, and glory!

Prayer

May my worship be pleasing in Your sight, dear God my Savior. I offer You my song of surrender and service—for You alone are worthy to be praised. I give You all that I am and that You will me to be. Thank You for all my blessings past, current, and to come. In Jesus's name, amen.

Declaration

I will forever lift God's name high
in worship and praise!

Live Again

Jesus was sleeping at the back of the boat with his head on a cushion. The disciples woke him up, shouting, "Teacher, don't you care that we're going to drown?" When Jesus woke up, he rebuked the wind and said to the waves, "Silence! Be still!" Suddenly the wind stopped, and there was a great calm (Mark 4:38-39 NLT).

HAVE YOU ALLOWED GOD to stand in the bow of your ship and speak peace to the thing that once terrified you? We can only benefit from resolved issues. The great tragedy is that most of us keep our pain active. Consequently, our power is never activated, because our past remains unresolved. If we want to see God's power come from the pain of an experience, we must allow the process of healing to take us far beyond bitterness into a resolution that releases us from the prison and sets us free.

God's healing process makes us free to taste life again, free to trust again, and free to live without the restrictive force of threatening fears. Someone may say, "I don't want to trust again." That is only because you are not healed. To never trust again is to live on the pinnacle of a tower. You are safe from life's threatening grasp, but you are so detached from life that you soon lose consciousness of people, places, dates, and events. You become locked into a time warp. You always talk about the past *because you stopped living years ago.* Listen to your speech. You discuss the past as if it were the present, because *the past has stolen the present* right out of your hand! In the name of Jesus, get it back!

Celebration is in order. Yes, it is time to celebrate—regardless of whether you've lost a marriage, a partnership, or a personal friend. Celebration is in order because you were split from your Siamese twin, and you are not dead. You are still alive! Are you ready to live, or do you still need to subject all your friends to a history class? Will you continue your incessant raging and blubbering about that which no one can change—the past?

I am trying to jump-start your heart and put you back into the presence of a real experience, far from the dank, dark valley of regret and remorse. It is easy to unconsciously live in a euphoric, almost historical mirage that causes current opportunities to evade you. Let it not be so.

Prayer

As You well know, Lord, I have been guilty of living in the past from time to time. Now, though, by Your power I will allow the process of total healing to take me far beyond bitterness into a mindset that releases me from prison and sets me free. With the Holy Spirit's guidance, I will celebrate the life You designed for me! In the name of the One who calms every storm, amen.

Declaration

I am ready to live again!

Everlasting Life

*Come to me with your ears wide open. Listen,
and you will find life. I will make an everlasting
covenant with you. I will give you all the unfailing
love I promised to David* (Isaiah 55:3 NLT).

ON OUR FINAL DAY TOGETHER, I don't want you to just close this devotional, put it on the shelf, and go back to living life as usual. I hope you received some good information, but most of all, I want to see you experience an impartation of the Lord's favor.

I pray these pages have served as your escort into the next level, your new dimension of spiritual blessing, abundance, and provision. I pray the Spirit of God whetted your appetite for new realms of glory, anointing, potential, and power that you didn't even know were inside you, waiting to be unlocked by each destiny-defining collision.

So here is my prayer for you—that the powerful hand of the Lord would come upon you, even now while you read these words. As the hand of the Lord was upon Elijah, and as the hand of the Lord was upon Elisha, I pray that you experience this same touch of power and favor that launches you into new and fruitful heights of service to God.

I pray that the powerful hand of the Lord would be upon every area of your life. That not one gift or talent would remain untouched. That not one ounce of potential would miss out.

The hand of the Lord is upon your house. The hand of the Lord is upon your business. The hand of the Lord is upon your ministry. The hand of the Lord is on your family. The hand of the Lord is on your schooling. The hand of the Lord is on your finances. The hand of the Lord is on your past. The hand of the Lord is on your debts. The hand of the Lord is upon you— His power works in you.

Let this be your prayer:

> Lord, whatever You're doing in the earth right now, don't do it without me. Favor me with Your power, and unlock the potential, the gifts, the talents, and the abilities within me. Orchestrate those destiny-defining appointments as only You can. Give me eyes to see what You're doing. Ears to hear You speaking. And a heart that responds to how You're moving in my life. I run toward everything You have for me, not looking back. Thank You, Father, for unlocking my purpose for Your glory in Jesus's name! Amen.

For God so loved the world that He gave His only begotten Son, that whoever believes in Him should not perish but have everlasting life (John 3:16 NKJV).

About T.D. Jakes

BISHOP T.D. JAKES is one of the world's most widely recognized pastors and a *New York Times* bestselling author of more than thirty books. Named by *Time* magazine as "America's Best Preacher," his message of healing and restoration is unparalleled, transcending cultural and denominational barriers.

Jakes is the founder and senior pastor of The Potter's House, which has a congregation of more than 30,000. His weekly television outreach, *The Potter's House,* and his daily television program, *The Potter's Touch,* have become favorites throughout America, Africa, Australia, Europe, and the Caribbean.

Bishop Jakes lives in Dallas, Texas, with his wife, Serita, five children, and two grandchildren.

Learn more about T.D. JAKES at

www.tdjakes.org
and
www.thepottershouse.org.

YOUR Prophetic COMMUNITY

Sign up for a **FREE** subscription to the Destiny Image digital magazine and get awesome content delivered directly to your inbox!

destinyimage.com/signup

Sign up for Cutting-Edge Messages that Supernaturally Empower You

- Gain valuable insights and guidance based on biblical principles
- Deepen your faith and understanding of God's plan for your life
- Receive regular updates and prophetic messages
- Connect with a community of believers who share your values and beliefs

Experience Fresh Video Content that Reveals Your Prophetic Inheritance

- Receive prophetic messages and insights
- Connect with a powerful tool for spiritual growth and development
- Stay connected and inspired on your faith journey

Listen to Powerful Podcasts that Propel You into God's Presence Every Day

- Deepen your understanding of God's prophetic assignment
- Experience God's revival power throughout your day
- Learn how to grow spiritually in your walk with God

In the Right Hands, This Book Will Change Lives!

Most of the people who need this message will not be looking for this book. To change their lives, you need to **put a copy of this book in their hands.**

Our ministry is constantly seeking methods to find the people who need this anointed message to change their lives. **Will you help us reach these people?**

Extend this ministry by sowing three, five, ten, or *even more* books today and change people's lives for the better! Your generosity will be part of catalyzing the Great Awakening that many have been prophesying and praying for.